The Nuts and Bolts of Surviving the Loss or Illness of a Loved One

A Step by Step Guide That Will Save Time and Money

Barbara T. Cochrane, B.S. and
Helen F. McGrane, Ph.D.

REGENESIS PUBLISHING
BURBANK, CALIFORNIA

The Nuts and Bolts of Surviving the Loss of a Loved One. A Step by Step Guide That Will Save Time and Money.

Published by Regenesis Publishing
P.O. Box 11353, Burbank, CA 91510-1353, U.S.A.
First Printing, 1990. Information provided in this book, especially the legal and financial advice, is presented for guidance only. It is not intended to substitute for the advice and counsel of professionals. Although accurate at the time of publication, the authors and publisher do not assume liability for errors or omissions arising out of future changes in law and/or economic circumstances.

Cover Design by Douglas J. Cochrane
10 9 8 7 6 5 4 3 2 1

Library of Congress Cataloguing-in-Publication Data

Cochrane, Barbara T.,
The nuts and bolts of surviving the loss or illness of a loved one: a step by step guide that will save time and money / Barbara T. Cochrane and Helen F. McGrane.
p. cm.
Includes index.
ISBN 0-9625863-3-1 :
1. Decedents' estate--United States--Popular works.
2. Survivors benefits--United States--Popular works.
3. Death--Psychological aspects--Popular works. 4. Finance, Personal--United States--Popular works. I. McGrane, Helen F., . II. Title. KF753.Z9C63 1990
640--dc20

89-64320
CIP

Table of Contents

INTRODUCTION

We confess to confusion, frustration and yes - anger after the loss of our respective family members. Who are we? Barbara is a health educator by profession, a wife, and mother of two adult children. Helen's background is in the health sciences with the present emphasis on education. She is also the mother of three adult children.

Barbara's mother died after an illness in which a nursing home became necessary. Helen's husband died after a three year struggle with cancer. We both did some preliminary planning during the illnesses of our respective family members. Yet, neither of us felt we had an organized approach that would have helped us avoid the mass of confusing paper and/or the frustrations that followed the deaths in our families.

As we dealt with details, we searched for reference texts that would assist us. We found a variety of texts, but no one organized document that could give us the guidance or the answers we sought. This book is the text we had hoped to find.

It is written to guide you and your family through the inevitable in all of our lives. It is a planning tool. It is also written for family members who must do the work involved after the death of a loved one. The emphasis is on the practical - the nuts and bolts of surviving a loss. We hope that you will find it useful.

DEDICATION

This book is dedicated to:

* our deceased family members, Aris Torigian and Vincent McGrane who inspired us to write this book,

* Barbara's husband Joseph, and her two children, Victoria and Doug, who had so much patience,

* Helen's three children, Ellen, Chris, and Connie, who provided encouragement,

* the host of people who have suffered with us as we have journeyed in our grief, and

* the people who will benefit by using the guidance of this book to answer their own vital questions.

PREFACE

Prepared or not, immediately after a death occurs, there is a need to make funeral arrangements, handle matters dealing wlth property, pay bills, pay taxes on property and/or file returns along with hundreds of other matters. The following questions are just a few that must be considered:

- Is there a family lawyer?
- Who pays inheritance taxes?
- Must I file for probate or can that be by-passed?
- Are there any heirlooms/collectibles?
- Is there a will?
- Where will I find a copy of the will?
- Is there a safe deposit box? Who has access to it?
- Was there any prior estate planning?

If you attempt to deal with all these matters during a time of emotional upheaval, thousands of dollars may be spent on fees for professional services that could have been saved. Through the use of this publication, survivors can conserve their assets. This can be done either through prior assistance provided by the reader as you organize your affairs or through research and the assistance provided by family and friends after the death has occurred.

Although completion of the working guide may seem overwhelming at first glance, applicable sections may be completed in a short and precise manner. The working guide is also cross-referenced for additional information and/or reference.

GUIDE THROUGH THE COMMUNICATION JUNGLE

Tips to simplify your tasks:

- Use this book as you communicate by phone, letter or in person. (You will have most of the vital information at your fingertips. Others often cooperate more fully when you value their time.)

- Try to organize your thoughts before you request information. Sometimes it helps to write out the points you wish to cover, the requested information, or possible referrals. (The shorter your statement, the more cooperative most people are.)

- Be prepared to repeat the same information each time you speak to a new person. (Written reminders make this easier.)

- Always ask the person's name and give them yours. Write the name down and use this in your conversation. If you are being transferred to another department, ask the telephone number or extension. (Knowing the correct person and telephone number eliminates the need to start all over again.) Keep notes for future reference.

- Ask what will be required to ensure prompt completion of the task at hand. (Guidance from an agency representative will often shorten or eliminate unnecessary steps and gain more cooperation from the agency.)

- When you are directed to call a company, government agency, etc., to get more information, ask for the exact spelling and for the telephone number. (Often it is assumed that a name familiar to one is familiar to all. However, if your efforts are complicated by incorrect spelling, or trying to locate a name that is not in your local directory, the problem of frustration is added to your bewildering list of things to do.)

- Never feel embarrassed to ask for more assistance or for needed clarification if you do not understand the problem or are not sure if you heard correctly. (Take control of the situation so you will not feel helpless, defeated or have undue self-pity. You are entitled to request the assistance needed to control your life. "Little victories" will help you along the road to self-sufficiency.)

- Ask questions. Do not be intimidated! If you do not understand, stop everything and get an answer ! (This can help you prevent unnecessary and costly errors that are difficult to correct.)

WORKING GUIDE

It is extremely important to maintain a current record of everything you own so that survivors (executors, family and friends) will not overlook items of value because they are unaware of their existence or worth. To make them aware of your assets and liabilities, you need to provide them with information contained in a Letter of Instruction or similar summary of information.

A Letter of Instruction is a valuable aid for anyone who wants to carry out your wishes. It provides your survivors with a measure of control in their stressful time of grief. Rather than a formal Letter of Instruction, this Working Guide defines the required information in an informal and organized manner. Since the Working Guide may be used as a legal document, the Guide should be dated and signed. See page 40.

*Decisions discussed in this book will **have** to be made by someone. If not by you, will you be satisfied with the decisions made by someone else on your behalf? For the choices YOU desire, take charge NOW by completing the essential information that applies to you.*

PERTINENT INFORMATION AND INCOME RESOURCES

My legal name:______________________________

Birth date:______________________________

Legal residence:______________________________

Place of birth:______________________________

Location of birth certificate:____________________

Religious affiliation:________________________

Clergy/phone#:______________________________

Uniform Donor Letter location:________________ (p. 131)

Life insurance policy(s)/annuity(s) are listed on page 25.

Employer to contact re profit sharing, pension plan, accident insurance, life insurance and other benefits:_______________

____

Phone #:____

Contact person:____

Veterans Administration (lump sum plus monthly):__________
Social Security resources are listed on page 11.

VETERANS ADMINISTRATION & SOCIAL SECURITY MUST BE NOTIFIED IN THE EVENT OF DEATH!

From other sources (Military, Civil Service, etc.):____________

____

Serial #:____

Rank or Rating:____

Meaningful service related infomation:____________________

____

If married, date and location of marriage:__________________

____

If widowed, date and location of spouse's death:_____________

____

I am the beneficiary/co-trustee of the___________________ trust. It is a (type)_________________________________ trust, and is established in the state of____________________. Trust Officer/Trustee is_____________________________________ and may be reached at (phone # & address):_______________

____.

I have designated____________________________as Executor/ Administrator of my estate in my will. He/she may be reached at____.

REPEAT ALL OF THE ABOVE FOR SPOUSE/OTHER

My legal name:______________________________________

Birth date:____

Legal residence:_____________________________________

Place of birth:____

Location of birth certificate:___________________________

Religious affiliation:_________________________________

Clergy/phone#:______________________________________

Uniform Donor Letter location:__________________________
____(p. 131)

Life insurance policy(s)/annuity(s) are listed on page 25.

Employer to contact re profit sharing, pension plan, accident insurance, life insurance and other benefits:__________________
____

Phone #:____

Contact person:______________________________________

Veterans Administration(lump sum plus monthly):_________

Social Security resources are listed on page 11.

VETERANS ADMINISTRATION & SOCIAL SECURITY MUST BE NOTIFIED IN THE EVENT OF DEATH!

From other sources (Military, Civil Service, etc.):____________
____

Serial #:______________________________

Rank or Rating:______________________________

Meaningful service related infomation:______________________________

____

If married, date and location of marriage:______________________________

____

If widowed, date and location of spouse's death:______________________________

____

I am the beneficiary/co-trustee of the______________________________

trust. It is a (type)______________________________

trust, and is established in the state of______________________________

Trust Officer/Trustee is______________________________

and may be reached at (phone # & address):______________________________

______________________________.

I have designated______________________________as Executor/ Administrator of my estate in my will. He/she may be reached at______________________________.

FIRST THINGS THAT SHOULD BE ATTENDED TO IN CASE OF DEATH

Call______________________________at______________________________

to help. Notify my employer/business associate at______________________________

______________________________.

Call my clergy; see pages 1 & 3. Make arrangements with the funeral home designated on page 35 & 38. For alternative preference of final rites, please see page 35 & 38. I have a

Uniform Donor's Card in my wallet: yes ❐ no ❐ , and a copy of the Uniform Donor Letter located at/in_____________________

____.

☞ *Request a minimum of ten copies of the death certificate. The Funeral Director will acquire them for you, or you may acquire them through the Bureau of Vital Statistics. (See page 130.)*

Call my attorney (name & phone #):_____________________

____

Call my Trust Officer (if appropriate):_____________________

____

Contact Social Security office at:_____________________

____

Obtain my insurance policies and begin the process of notification. (All Insurance policies/annuities may not be needed for immediate cash.) Contact my agent or____________ at______________________________for advice on insurance matters. For location of immediately accessible funds (checking account/cash/etc.), please refer to page 15.

THINGS TO DO WHEN DEATH IS IMMINENT

GIVE SUPPORT TO THE DYING PERSON. PROVIDE DIGNITY. Notify other family members and/or significant others. Call a member of the clergy. (See above.)

Complete vital information and/or update this Working Guide.

Obtain access to funds that will be required for on-going business as well as medical care. (Check with Executor/ Administrator or attorney for assistance.)

See if Uniform Donor Card exists and alert others who will be affected.

Call____________________at____________to help.

Notify my employer (company)________________.

Phone #__________________. Notify the bank that holds home mortgage if payments will be affected or landlord if residence will be unoccupied. See pages 32 - 34.

Bank:____________________Phone #:__________

Landlord:__________________Phone #:__________

If a change of address is required, contact the Post Office for Change of Address forms. If continuing bills, utilities, medical bills need attention, see page 9. For location of immediately accessible funds (checking account/cash/etc.), please see page 15. Notify estate Executor/Administrator ________________________ at ________________.

Durable Power of Attorney for Health Care is held by ________________________ at ____________.

Location of Power of Attorney____________________

____.

Children: *If minor children are involved, name guardian and/ or alternate guardian, and relationship to testator*

____.

Full name:____

Date & location of birth:______________________________

Address:____

Full name:____

Date & location of birth:______________________________

Address:____

Full name:____

Date & location of birth:______________________________

Address:____

Full name:____

Date & location of birth:______________________________

Address:____

Family Members: Mother, Father, and siblings and/or next of kin. It is important to list even if they are no longer living. (You may wish to list close personal friends.)

Full name:____

Date & location of birth:______________________________

Address:____

Full name:____

Date & location of birth:______________________________

Address:____

Full name:______________________________________

Date & location of birth:____________________________

Address:____

Full name:______________________________________

Date & location of birth:____________________________

Address:____

Full name:______________________________________

Date & location of birth:____________________________

Address:____

☞ *Read through ALL the Working Guide to familiarize yourself with all the sources of information that are already available, and to learn what you will need to complete if the information is not already in place.*

ONGOING BUSINESS

Establish joint checking accounts when possible, in order to pay obligated debts.

Household Bills | Company Name | Phone#

Cable service:__________________________________

Electricity:__________________________________

Gas Company:__________________________________

Gardener/Lawncare:______________________________

Housekeeper:__________________________________

Newspapers:__________________________________

Pest Control:__________________________________

Pool Maintenance:______________________________

Security Systems Co.:____________________________

Telephone Co.(Local):____________________________

Telephone Co.(Long Distance):______________________

Veterinarian:__________________________________

Medical Bills

(Ask suppliers to submit bills directly to Medicare, if this is appropriate.)

Payment forms available from:______________________

Medicare contact (Tollfree #):______________________

Medicare #:__________________________________

ADDITIONAL ONGOING BILLS THAT MUST BE PAID

such as insurance policies, mortgage, rent, taxes, etc.

____

____

____

____

____

____

____

☞ *If the safe deposit box needs to be accessed, you will need to fill out a new card with the additional name to attend to matters during illness. Please see page 12. Now is the time to complete this information.*

If the illness does not allow prompt return home and an alternative care facility is required, ask the doctor, friends or the local hospital for resources. Call and ask to visit the potential alternative housing site. If a professional live-in will suffice, obtain names from the same sources. See page 76

Name of facility:______________________________

Contact person:______________________________

Phone #:______________Address:______________

Name of facility:______________________________

Contact person:______________________________

Phone #:______________Address:______________

Name of facility:______________________________

Contact person:______________________________

Phone #:______________Address:______________

Name of facility:____

Contact person:____

Phone #:________________Address:______________________

Name of facility:____

Contact person:____

Phone #:________________Address:______________________

Name of facility:____

Contact person:____

Phone #:________________Address:______________________

Medical transportation services available locally:

Support groups & resources:

See page 103
These are available for the terminally ill patient and family.

SOCIAL SECURITY

See page 48
Name (1):____

Social Security Card #:____________________________

Name (2):____________________________________

Social Security Card #:____________________________

Location of card(s) and last earnings report(s):____________

____

☞ *File claims immediately to avoid loss of benefit check(s). Social Security will NOT pay retroactively.*

Call the local Social Security office for an appointment.They will tell you what you will need to bring with you.

Phone #:________________________

Address of office:_________________________________

Expect a lump sum of about $__________. Additional benefits may be paid to eligible family members.

SAFE DEPOSIT BOX *Some States must by law seal the owner's box in the event of death, even if jointly owned. Be aware of your own situation.* See page 86

Bank:__________________Address:___________________

Phone #:________________

Bank:__________________Address:___________________

Phone #:________________

In whose name(s):__________________________________

(Give alias, if used.)

Number of box(es):______________ ________________

Key location:______________________________________

List pertinent contents:______________________________

____

Individual(s) with access: ______________________________

____

POST OFFICE BOX

Address: ______________________________________

Owners: ______________________________________

Number: ____________ Location of key/combination: ______

____

BUSINESS (Either have interest in, or wholly owned)

Name of business: ______________________________

Address: ______________________________________

Type of partnership: ____________________________

Co-owner: ____________________________________

Name of business: ______________________________

Address: ______________________________________

Type of partnership: ____________________________

Co-owner: ____________________________________

Brief description of business: ______________________

____

____

LOCATION OF VITAL DOCUMENTS

Last will and testament: __________________________

Dated/Updated: ________________________________

Uniform Donor Card and Letter (organ & body donation):______

____

Birth & baptismal certificates:______________________

Confirmation (religious certificates):_________________

Credit card(s) list & card(s):______________________

Diplomas (school/tech. school):____________________

Insurance policies:___________________________

Investment certificates:_________________________

Marriage certificate(s):_________________________

Divorce/Annulment/Separation papers:______________

Family documents:____________________________

IRA/Keogh/pension papers:_______________________

Military records:_____________________________

Naturalization papers:__________________________

Passports:_________________________________

Power of Attorney (general & health):_______________

____

Real estate deed(s):___________________________

Safe deposit box inventory & key(s):________________

Social Security card(s):_________________________

Tax records:________________________________

Trusts (type & for the benefit of):__________________

____

Vehicle title(s):______________________________

Other (adoption, contracts, business documents, etc.):______

____

See page 55

CHECKING ACCOUNTS

Designate joint owners, community property, individual, business, etc.

Name of firm:______________________________

Account #:______________________________

Address:______________________________

Name(s) on account:______________________________

Kind of account:______________________________

Name of firm:______________________________

Account #:______________________________

Address:______________________________

Name(s) on account:______________________________

Kind of account:______________________________

Name of firm:______________________________

Account #:______________________________

Address:______________________________

Name(s) on account:______________________________

Kind of account:______________________________

☞ *Repeat to cover all accounts. See page 107 for additional accounts. Cancelled checks are an excellent resource for survivors, as are old check registers.*

See page 57

SAVINGS ACCOUNTS/CERTIFICATES OF DEPOSIT MONEY MARKET ACCOUNTS

(Location of immediately accessible funds)
*Indicate with an * if an IRA, Keogh or Tax-deferred account.*

Name of facility:____________________

Account #:____________________

Address:____________________

Name(s) on account:____________________

Type of account:____________________

Location of passbook or certificate:____________________

Maturity date (in pencil):____________________

Special instructions/information:____________________

Beneficiary:____________________

Name of facility:____________________

Account #:____________________

Address:____________________

Name(s) on account:____________________

Type of account:____________________

Location of passbook or certificate:____________________

Maturity date (in pencil):____________________

Special instructions/information:____________________

Beneficiary:____________________

See page 108 for additional accounts.

DOCTORS

See page 70

Indicate Doctor's specialty after name.

Doctor:____________________

Address:____

Phone#:____

Doctor:____

Address:____

Phone#:____

Doctor:____

Address:____

Phone#:____

Pediatrician:____

Address:____

Phone#:____

Dentist:____

Address:____

Phone#:____

Children's Dentist:____

Address:____

Phone#:____

Usual Medical Care Facility:____

Address:____

Phone#:____

See page 133 Location of Letter of Consent for Medical Care of Children:

____

____

See page 109 for additional listings.

ATTORNEY

See page 78

Name(s):____

Associated with (firm):______________________________

Address:____

Phone #:____

ACCOUNTANT / CPA

See page 59

Name(s):____

Associated with (firm):______________________________

Address:____

Phone #:____

FINANCIAL PLANNER / ADVISOR

See page 61

Name(s):____

Associated with (firm):______________________________

Address:____

Phone #:____

CREDIT CARDS

See page 68

*Indicate credit/life insurance with *.*

Company:_______________________________________

Address:____

Phone #:____

Card #:____

Company:_______________________________________

Address:____

Phone #:____

Card #:____

Company:______________________________________

Address:_______________________________________

Phone #:____

Card #:____

Company:______________________________________

Address:_______________________________________

Phone #:____

Card #:____

Company:______________________________________

Address:_______________________________________

Phone #:____

Card #:____

See page 110 for additional listings.

LIABILITIES

Debts owed by me (vehicle, personal, business, etc.)

*Indicate credit/life insurance with *.*

Owed to:______________________________________

Address:______________________________________

Name(s) on loan:________________________________

Account #:_____________________________________

Monthly payment:_______________________________

Location of papers:______________________________

Collateral, if any:______________________________

Owed to:______________________________

Address:______________________________

Name(s) on loan:______________________________

Account #:______________________________

Monthly payment:______________________________

Location of papers:______________________________

Collateral, if any:______________________________

Owed to:______________________________

Address:______________________________

Name(s) on loan:______________________________

Account #:______________________________

Monthly payment:______________________________

Location of papers:______________________________

Collateral, if any:______________________________

See page 111 for additional listings.

ASSETS

Debts owed to me (vehicle, personal, business, etc.)

Debtor:______________________________

Address:______________________________

Description of debt:______________________________

Terms:______________________________

Balance (in pencil):______________________________

Location of documents:______________________________

Debtor:____

Address:______________________________________

Description of debt:______________________________

Terms:____

Balance (in pencil):______________________________

Location of documents:___________________________

See page 112 for additional listings.

OTHER INCOME PRODUCING ASSETS

Patents, copyrights, trusts, partnerships, proprietorships, close corporations, etc.

Asset:____

Amount of annual income:_________________________

Due date:______________________________________

Asset:____

Amount of annual income:_________________________

Due date:______________________________________

Asset:____

Amount of annual income:_________________________

Due date:______________________________________

Asset:____

Amount of annual income:_________________________

Due date:______________________________________

VEHICLES

If the registered owner is unable to drive, contact the insurance company concerning liability of any additional drivers.

Make, Model, Year:______________________________

Body type:____________________Color:____________

Registered to:__________________________________

Identification #:________________________________

Location of title:________________________________

Serviced at:____________________________________

Insured by:____________________________________

Phone #:______________________________________

Extended warranty: ❐ yes ❐ no

Location of policy:_______________________________

Make, Model, Year:______________________________

Body type:____________________Color:____________

Registered to:__________________________________

Identification #:________________________________

Location of title:________________________________

Serviced at:____________________________________

Insured by:____________________________________

Phone #:______________________________________

Extended warranty: ❐ yes ❐ no

Location of policy:_______________________________

See page 59 ☞

INCOME TAX RETURNS

Old returns are an excellent resource for information.

Location of all previous returns:______________________

____

____

____

____

Tax preparer (Accountant or Financial Planner):____________

____

Phone #:____

Are taxes paid on a quarterly basis? ❒ yes ❒ no

If so, where are forms located?______________________

____

Does tax preparer have copies of previous returns?

❒ yes ❒ no

If so, date of earliest return:______________________

See page 63

INVESTMENTS - *Indicate with * if investment is an IRA/ KEOUGH/ RETIREMENT PLAN. For jointly-held accounts, you should keep accurate records that show whose funds were deposited. Tax consequences will often depend on whose funds were deposited and when. Your good record keeping can reduce taxes.*

Stocks *(currently held)*

Company:____

Name(s) on certificate:______________________________

Number of shares:__________Certificate number(s):________

____

Purchase date(s) and price(s):______________________

Location of certificate(s):________________________

Held in street name? ❐ yes ❐ no

Company:______________________________________

Name(s) on certificate:___________________________

Number of shares:__________Certificate number(s):________

____

Purchase date(s) and price(s):______________________

Location of certificate(s):________________________

Held in street name? ❐ yes ❐ no

Additional listings on page 113.

Bonds / Notes / Bills *(currently held)*

Issuer:_______________________________________

Issued to:_____________________________________

Maturity date:_________________________________

Location of the certificate:_______________________

Held in street name? ❐ yes ❐ no

Additional listings on page 114.

Other Investments - *US Savings Bonds, government securities, etc . For each of these investments. list amount, to whom issued, issuer and maturity date. List the location of the certificates. See page 115 for additional listings.*

The following securities are pledged against loans or margined:

____

____

They are held by (names & addresses):____________________

____

____

My broker:__________________________Phone #:_____________

Address:____

____

Account #:____

List additional broker(s)/brokerage house(s):________________

____

____

See page 52

LIFE INSURANCE/ANNUITIES

To collect benefits, a copy of the death certificate should be sent to each company. Additional benefits may be available through group policies i .e. . labor unions, fraternal organizations or employer.

Full name of insured:__________________________________

Owner of policy:______________________________________

Insurance company:___________________________________

Amount:___________________Kind of policy:__________________

Policy #:________________________Disability option ❐ yes ❐ no

Beneficiaries:____

Issue date:______________________Maturity date:______________

Method of payout (or options):____________________________

Full name of insured:__________________________________

Owner of policy:______________________________

Insurance company:______________________________

Amount:______________ Kind of policy:______________

Policy #:__________________ Disability option ❒ yes ❒ no

Beneficiaries:______________________________

Issue date:________________ Maturity date:__________

Method of payout (or options):____________________

Full name of insured:__________________________

Owner of policy:______________________________

Insurance company:______________________________

Amount:______________ Kind of policy:______________

Policy #:__________________ Disability option ❒ yes ❒ no

Beneficiaries:______________________________

Issue date:________________ Maturity date:__________

Method of payout (or options):____________________

Location of policies:__________________________

For veteran's insurance in the amount of ____________, call ______________ at the Veterans Administration. Policy # is __________________, with ____ as the beneficiaries.

For additional Insurance/Annuity listings, see page 116.

OTHER INSURANCE POLICIES

Accident

Company:________________________Address:____________

____

Policy #:________________________Coverage:_____________

Beneficiary:____

Agent:_______________________Location of policy:__________

____

Company:________________________Address:____________

____

Policy #:________________________Coverage:_____________

Beneficiary:____

Agent:_______________________Location of policy:__________

____

Home/Condo/ Co-op/ Income Property (Indicate with * if the household contents are covered along with the structure.)

Coverage:____________________________Property Address:

____

Company:________________________Address:____________

____

Policy #:_______________________Location of policy:__________

____

Term (renewal date):____________Agent:___________________

Coverage:______________________________Property Address:

____

Company:__________________________Address:_____________

____

Policy #:_______________________Location of policy:_________

____

Term (renewal date):___________Agent:___________________

Coverage:______________________________Property Address:

____

Company:__________________________Address:_____________

____

Policy #:_______________________Location of policy:_________

____

Term (renewal date):___________Agent:___________________

Coverage:______________________________Property Address:

____

Company:__________________________Address:_____________

____

Policy #:_______________________Location of policy:_________

____

Term (renewal date):___________Agent:___________________

Medical

Coverage:________________________Insured:_______________

Company:_________________________Address:____________

____

Policy #:______________________Location of policy:_________

____

Through employer/ other group:___________________________

Agent:_____________Personal/Family coverage:____________

Coverage:________________Insured:_______________________

Company:_________________________Address:____________

____

Policy #:______________________Location of policy:_________

____

Through employer/ other group:___________________________

Agent:_____________Personal/Family coverage:____________

Coverage:_________________Insured:______________________

Company:_________________________Address:____________

____

Policy #:______________________Location of policy:_________

____

Through employer/ other group:___________________________

Agent:_____________Personal/Family coverage:____________

Additional listings on page 117.

Disability

Company:________________________Address:____________

____

Insured:_______________________Policy #:______________

Policy location:______________________Amount:___________

Company:________________________Address:____________

____

Insured:_______________________Policy #:______________

Policy location:______________________Amount:___________

Liability (personal and/or professional)

Company:_____________________Address:_______________

____

Insured:_____________________Policy #:________________

Policy location:______________________Amount:___________

Company:_____________________Address:_______________

____

Insured:_____________________Policy #:________________

Policy location:______________________Amount:___________

REAL ESTATE - House/ Condo/ Co-op/ Income property

See page 74

Title is held by (names):________________________________

Address:____

Lot:__________Block:___________Assessor description:_____

____

Deed location:____

Real Estate agent:___________________Phone #:_____________

Property Management by:________________________________

Monthly Association dues:___________Payable to:___________

____

File on property located (deed/title insurance/lease agreement, etc.):____

Title is held by (names):________________________________

Address:____

Lot:__________Block:___________Assessor description:______

____

Deed location:____

Real Estate agent :__________________Phone #:_____________

Property Management by:________________________________

Monthly Association dues:___________Payable to:___________

____

File on property located (deed/title insurance/lease agreement, etc.):____

Title is held by (names):________________________________

Address:____

Lot:__________Block:___________Assessor description:_____

____

Deed location:____

Real Estate agent:____________________Phone #:______________

Property Management by:____________________________________

Monthly Association dues:___________Payable to:___________

____

File on property located (deed/title insurance/lease agreement, etc.):____

Title is held by (names):___________________________________

Mortgage(s)

Property location:____

Held by:_________________________Address:________________

____

Loan #:___________________ Payment due:__________________

Amount of original mortgage:____________Balloon:_________

Date loan began:____________Final payment due:___________

Location of payment booklet/statements:___________________

Second mortgage held by:___________________________________

Address:____

Loan #:___________________ Payment due:__________________

Amount of second mortgage:_____________Balloon:_________

Date loan began:____________Final payment due:___________

Location of payment booklet/statements:___________________

Life insurance on mortgage: ❐ yes ❐ no

Policy#:______________Policy location:______________________

Property location:____

Held by:_________________________Address:________________

Loan #:__________________ Payment due:__________________

Amount of original mortgage:____________ Balloon:_________

Date loan began:____________ Final payment due:___________

Location of payment booklet / statements:___________________

Second mortgage held by:_________________________________

Address:____

Loan #:__________________ Payment due:__________________

Amount of second mortgage:_____________ Balloon:_________

Date loan began:____________ Final payment due:___________

Location of payment booklet / statements:___________________

Life insurance on mortgage: ❒ yes ❒ no

Policy #:________________ Policy location:__________________

Property location:____

Held by:_________________________ Address:_________________

Loan #:__________________ Payment due:__________________

Amount of original mortgage:____________ Balloon:_________

Date loan began:____________ Final payment due:___________

Location of payment booklet / statements:___________________

Second mortgage held by:_________________________________

Address:____

Loan #:__________________ Payment due:__________________

Amount of second mortgage:_____________ Balloon:_________

Date loan began:____________ Final payment due:___________

Location of payment booklet / statements:___________________

Life insurance on mortgage: ❒ yes ❒ no

Policy #:________________Policy location:___________________

☞ *In the event of death, the unpaid balance will be paid if mortgage insurance is in force. Notify the bank immediately to receive prompt payment.*
This clears any unpaid balance on that piece of real estate.

If there is a Veteran's Exemption, the location of the papers for this documentation is:____________________________________

PROPERTY TAXES

Location of past bills:____________________________________

Paid annually/semi-annually (dates for each location):_____

____

COST OF REAL ESTATE

Initial purchase price:__________Cost to purchase:__________

Location of property:_____________________________________

Initial purchase price:__________Cost to purchase:__________

Location of property:_____________________________________

Initial purchase price:__________Cost to purchase:__________

Location of property:_____________________________________

ITEMIZED PROPERTY IMPROVEMENTS

This is important, as the initial price and upkeep of property are the basis when selling property.

Location of bills (note property location):___________________

See page 90

FINAL ARRANGEMENTS

Cemetery/ Funeral/ Memorial Society/ Cemetery Plot/ Vault/ Mausoleum Space

Final arrangements of: (1)______________________________.

Person authorized to make final arrangements (if other than immediate family):______________________________

Purchase date:__________________Deed #:__________________

Location:______________________________

Other information (Perpetual care, memorial plaque, marker, etc.): ______________________________

Preferred mortuary:__________________Address:__________

____

Type of service (Memorial, religious, etc.):__________________

Religion:______________Music/ Readings/ etc.:______________

____

Desired pallbearers:______________________________

In lieu of flowers request (if any):______________________________

Open or closed casket:________________Disposition of remains:

Cremation ❒ Burial ❒

☞ *When arranging a funeral, this book should be used when meeting with the Funeral Director. There will be* <u>*many*</u> *important facts for you to supply, and this is no time to rely on your memory, even if you know all the facts!*

Father's name and birthplace:______________________________

Mother's name (maiden) and birthplace:______________________

Resided in the state since:____________County:______________

In U.S.A. since:__________ Military service (branch):____________

Dates:__________________

☞ *Veterans' discharge papers may be required by Funeral Director.*

Occupation:______________________________ Retired?:________

Highest grade of school completed:__________________________

Meaningful accomplishments:_____________________________

Items and/or activities I would like included in my obituary:

____

____

____

Prepaid Funeral? ❒ yes ❒ no Through whom:_____________

Memorial Society? ❒ yes ❒ no Phone #:_________________

☞ *If you have arranged with a Funeral Director to apply life insurance proceeds toward funeral costs, take a copy of the policy with you when meeting with him/her. If the proceeds are greater than the cost of the funeral, arrange to cash policy prior to payment for funeral.*

Organizational Membership-Fraternal/Service/Other

*Mark an * if any insurance benefits exist.*

Organization:____________________ Member since:____________

Contact person:______________________ Phone #:____________

Organization:____________________ Member since:____________

Contact person:______________________ Phone #:____________

Organization:____________________ Member since:____________

Contact person:____________________Phone #:____________

Personal Possessions

Collection/ Artwork/ Jewelry/ China/ etc.

I would like to have the following people receive these items:

Item	Person

Instruction for disposition of other items is located at:_______

____

Additional special wishes - Memorial gifts/ desired post-service activities, etc.

____

____

____

Final arrangements of: (2)___________________________.

Person authorized to make final arrangements (if other than immediate family):___________________________

Purchase date:_____________Deed #:__________________

Location:______________________________________

Other information (Perpetual care, memorial plaque, marker, etc.):______________________________________

Preferred mortuary:__________________Address:__________

____

Type of service (Memorial, religious, etc.):_______________

Religion:_______________Music / Readings / etc.:__________

____

Desired pallbearers:__________________________________

In lieu of flowers request (if any):_______________________

Open or closed casket:_______________Disposition of remains:

Cremation ❒ Burial ❒

☞ *When arranging a funeral, this book should be used when meeting with the Funeral Director. There will be* <u>*many*</u> *important facts for you to supply, and this is no time to rely on your memory, even if you know all the facts!*

Father's name and birthplace:__________________________

Mother's name (maiden) and birthplace:___________________

Resided in the state since:____________County:_____________

In U.S.A. since:__________Military service (branch):____________

Dates:__________________

☞ *Veterans' discharge papers may be required by Funeral Director.*

Occupation:_____________________________Retired?:________

Highest grade of school completed:________________________

Meaningful accomplishments:___________________________

Items and/or activities I would like to include in my obituary:

____

____

____

Prepaid Funeral? ❒ yes ❒ no Through whom:____________

Memorial Society? ❒ yes ❒ no Phone #:______________

☞ *If you have arranged with a Funeral Director to apply life insurance proceeds toward funeral costs, take a copy of the policy with you when meeting with him/her. If the proceeds are greater than the cost of the funeral, arrange to cash policy prior to payment for funeral.*

Organizational Membership-Fraternal/Service/Other

*Mark an * if any insurance benefits exist.*

Organization:________________ Member since:__________

Contact person:__________________ Phone #:___________

Organization:________________ Member since:__________

Contact person:__________________ Phone #:___________

Organization:________________ Member since:__________

Contact person:__________________ Phone #:___________

Personal Possessions

Collection/ Artwork/ Jewelry/ China/ etc.

I would like to have the following people receive these items:

Item	Person

Item	Person

Instruction for disposition of other items is located at:________

____

____

Additional special wishes - Memorial gifts/ desired post-service activities, etc.

____

____

____

Date of Original Completion:__________Signature:______________

Update:____________Signature:____________________

Update:____________Signature:____________________

Update:____________Signature:____________________

"IMMEDIATE MATTERS"/ "ONGOING MATTERS"

"Immediate Matters" and "Ongoing Matters" have many overlapping areas. You will be referred to an appropriate section as this overlapping occurs. When a fuller explanation will be helpful, references are noted. As you read the sections below, it will become obvious that the more instructions are defined prior to death, the easier it will be for survivors to deal with the numerous business decisions that must be handled. Unfortunately, it is difficult if not impossible to prepare for the emotional issues after a death has occurred.

"Immediate Matters" will deal with the priorities immediately after a death has occurred while "Ongoing Matters" focuses upon the steps that may be taken during the course of a long term or final illness. Both sections require attention to personal, legal, and financial matters. It will help to keep your pencil handy and make notations in the Working Guide/ Letter of Instruction as you read this text.

"Immediate Matters"

1. If organ donation is desired, check with your physician, lawyer, and/or executor. See pages 1, 3 & 91.

2. Call the Funeral Director who will coordinate arrangements. See pages 35 & 38.

3. Notify persons and businesses that need to be aware of the death. See pages 4, 5 & 6.

4. Locate the will and other pertinent documents. See pages 12 & 13 for location of these documents.

5. If appropriate, call a member of the clergy to officiate at services and/or other needs of family/friends. See pages 1 & 3.

6. Contact an attorney. See pages 5 & 18.

7. Accessible funds will be needed immediately. See

pages 15 & 16 for location of funds and if someone is already able to access these funds.

8. Contact the local Post Office and have mail forwarded if the residence will be vacated. See item #5 under "Ongoing Matters."

9. Begin the process to acquire funds from insurance policies. Read Chapter on "Benefits" (p. 48-54) concerning the process and distribution alternatives for insurance funds. Also, see page 25.

10. Notify utility and service providers that service will be discontinued if the deceased lived alone. See page 9 for names and locations of companies.

11. Notify Estate Administrator/Executor. See page 6.

12. If Social Security, Veteran's Administration, etc. are to be notified, see pages 11, 48 & 51.

"Ongoing Matters"

If you have the benefit of assistance from the ill person, you may have the Working Guide already completed or begun by now. Do consider taping some of your conversations for valuable history and/or information about the family.

1. Notify clergy if appropriate. See pages 1 & 3.

2. Obtain a copy of the will for review. If desired or needed, update it. See #4 above.

3. Maintain payment of current bills, e.g., utility bills; insurance on life, health, property; rent/mortgage, vehicle loan installments; vehicle registration, etc.

4. If illness requires lengthy hospitalization and the residence will be empty, contact utilities to determine

what steps to take. There may be a lower rate for temporary non-use. See # 10 above.

5. This is a good time to contact the Post Office if mail needs to be forwarded. If a death has occurred you will need to complete a change of address card to have mail forwarded. See pages 13, 87 & 88.

6. To avoid tax penalties, do pay local, state and federal taxes in a timely manner. Consult your tax preparer if there is a need or possibility for filing an extension. See page 23.

7. Maintain credit card payments. Consider changing the account name or closing the account. See pages 18 & 124.

8. The registration of a vehicle can be changed prior to a death if a sale is needed for funds. A "pink slip" showing ownership, current registration and current smog certificate (for some states) will usually be required. Bring the document with you which establishes your relationship to the registered owner. See pages 14, 22 & 46.

9. Consider transfer of assets to minimize estate taxes and fees. This can be done so that there is still control during one's lifetime. See page 82.

10. Contact an attorney to determine whether there will be a need for an "Affidavit of Right" to transfer property or if property transfers directly via joint tenancy or a living trust to a surviving spouse. See page 82.

11. If death is imminent, you may need the contents of a safe deposit box. Names of authorized key holders can be provided by the bank. See pages 12 & 13.

12. Locate a source of any existing money reserves as expenses do continue. Establishing access to a checking and/or savings account will help you to deal with the many expenses that continue. You may not need to use

your own funds, and in any event, you should keep track of all expenses carefully. There will need to be an accounting in the settlement of the estate. Out of pocket expenses should be recorded, as these are usually reimbursed with the estate settlement. See page 15.

13. If there have been investments, there may be on going concerns to be managed. Find out the maturity date of any Certificates of Deposit, and determine if funds should be reinvested, and/or are needed for current expenses. Also, there may be proxies and additional decisions that require contact with an investment broker, your real estate broker, and/or financial planner. See pages 15, 18, 25 & 30.

14. If you do not drive and have been dependent on others for your transportation, you should seriously consider driving lessons. A vehicle may be the main source of your independence. Do not let "kind" family/ friends dissuade you. There are driving schools that specialize in the instruction of the mature non-driver. You are never too old to learn to drive if you desire to do so.

15. Ask medical service suppliers to submit bills directly to your insurance company or Medicare. This has the advantage that you do not spend your money needlessly while reimbursement is pending. It also gets a faster response to the provider. Emphasize that you are not asking for reduced fees, just direct billing. Then, be prompt with the balance. Maintain communication with the provider to ensure that bills are not sent for collection. See pages 9 & 16.

16. If your family member or friend is receiving care outside the home, maintain a high profile so that caretakers are aware of your presence. The quality of care tends to be more consistent when there are frequent visits by family and/or friends. See page 10.

17. When you have appointments with medical personnel, legal counsel, financial advisors, etc, it helps to be accompanied by a trusted friend or family member. They become a valuable ally in asking questions, verifying information, etc.

18. Contact the deceased's place of employment to determine if you qualify for continuing medical insurance coverage. Confirm what process will be necessary.

19. Following a death, use caution removing <u>any</u> contents from the deceased's home. This is the Executor/ Administrator's responsibility. Premature removal of property or effects may cause future problems.

WHEN YOU NEED HELP

Whether you are faced with the prospect of losing a loved one, or have already experienced the loss, it is often difficult to think as clearly as you normally would. We suggest that you ask for help from family, friends, or agencies to ease some of the inevitable problems and help you find solutions.

Sometimes the most obvious support groups are the easiest to overlook. Various fraternal organizations and clubs have resources; your house of worship may have dedicated assistance for you. If there has been a hospitalization, check to see if they offer bereavement or support groups. In many communities, there are support groups for almost every type of illness or disability. There are a variety of resources that are also available from local, State, and Federal agencies. The personnel in these groups and agencies are usually well trained and anxious to be helpful.

If you have not learned to drive a car, and you find yourself without transportation, this is the time to consider learning to drive! There are special Driver Education courses that are designed especially for the mature driver. Do not decide that you are too old or too anxious without checking out this resource. You will want to encourage your sense of being in charge of yourself! A Car Care class is helpful if you have been dependent upon someone else for this task. Auto Mechanics are encouraged to provide reliable efficient service when a car owner is knowledgeable and wants a well maintained car. The Automobile Association of America (AAA) has classes available or can provide referrals for this type of class. Also, most insurance companies provide a discount on the premium for policyholders who are 55 or older if you take one of these classes and are a good driver.

You might want to learn what services are available at local Multipurpose Centers. Frequently, they have counseling; nutrition; financial advice; legal services; housing information; work and volunteer opportunities; health information; educational classes; transportation; and multi-lingual referrals. There may be Senior Day Care available and/or Home

Delivered meals for those who are unable to care for themselves completely, but are not interested in a Continuing Care Community.

It is important not to suffer in silence or alone. Check your telephone directory under social services, welfare agencies, family services, the American Red Cross, Social Security and/ or Veterans' Administration. You'll find that one or more of them will have services that are of benefit to you. It really is surprising. Now the hard part -- take the steps; make the telephone calls that will make these services work for you.

Sometimes the answer to a simple question seems impossible to find -- especially when you are seeking that answer from the Federal Government. However, you will be happy to know that there is a staff of carefully selected and trained people who can help you get information from more than 125 Government agencies. The Federal Information Center is as close as your telephone, and often is a toll-free number. The staff can answer questions quickly and efficiently, or help you find the correct office for the answer. You can find this resource by looking in your telephone directory under United States Federal Government, Federal Information Center.

BENEFITS

SOCIAL SECURITY

Cash benefits from Social Security are dependent upon the credit that has been established for work performed while covered under Social Security. The amount of credit for time worked depends upon age and/or whether the individual was disabled. More information about the exact requirements is available at any Social Security office. To find the address of the nearest office, look in the phone directory under Government Offices, subheading,Health and Human Services.

ELIGIBILITY (Requirements may vary due to legislative changes. Check eligibility updates with Social Security Office.)

A. Monthly Benefits
Social Security Survivor monthly benefits are provided to the following surviving dependents:

(1) Unmarried children under age 18 (or under 19 if fulltime high school students).

(2) Unmarried children 18 or over who were severely disabled before the age of 22 and who remain disabled.

(3) Surviving spouse age 60 or older (which may require that the worker was fully insured).

(4) Surviving spouse or surviving divorced mother or father if the latter is caring for the deceased's child under 16 (or disabled) who is getting a benefit based on the earnings of a deceased worker.

(5) Surviving spouse age 50 or older who becomes disabled not later than seven years after the worker's death, or within seven years after mother or father's benefits end.

(6) Dependent parents 62 or older (if the individual had been fully insured). Proof of dependency for more than one half of their support is required to be filed within two years of the death, even though the deceased is not of retirement age.

(7) Surviving divorced spouse at age 60 or disabled surviving divorced spouse 50 or older if the marriage lasted 10 years or more (if the deceased worker was fully insured).

(8) Children may be eligible for benefits based on a grandparent's earnings if the natural parents are disabled or deceased, and if the grandchildren are living with and are supported by the grandparents. This requires that the deceased had been currently or fully insured.

B. Lump Sum Benefit
A lump sum death benefit is payable after the death of an insured person to the following individuals:

(1) The spouse who was living in the same household as the deceased at the time of death.

(2) A spouse not living in the same household, who was eligible for or entitled to monthly benefits based on the deceased's record at the time of death.

(3) A child or children of the deceased who were eligible for or entitled to monthly benefits based on the deceased's record at the time of death.

A lump sum payment may be available to an individual, other than a dependent, who assumes responsibility for burial expenses. Check with Social Security.

☞ *Application for the lump sum benefit MUST be made within two years following the death of the worker. (Do not delay because you do not have all the proofs of relationship. Substitute proof documents may also be accepted.)*

C. Some or All of the Following Documents May Be Needed to Support a Claim For Death Benefits:

(1) Employment record of deceased for the most recent calendar year (W-2 form or income tax return).

(2) Birth certificates of minor children.

(3) Birth certificate of widow, if age 60 or over, or disabled widow if age 50 or over.

(4) Copy of marriage certificate (when applying for widow's monthly benefits).

(5) Death certificate.

(6) Social Security card or record of deceased's Social Security number.

(7) Receipted funeral bill .

D. Medicare

If you are eligible for Social Security as a surviving dependent, you are eligible for hospital insurance protection when you are 65. This offers basic protection against the costs of hospital and related care plus a voluntary supplementary program covering the costs of doctor's services and other items and services not covered under the basic program. It is good to apply for Medicare three months before your birthday month. Protection will then start at 65. More information about Medicare is available at your local Social Security office.

E. Confirmation of Social Security Earnings.

It is a good idea to check earning records every three years to make sure earnings are correctly reported and recorded. You may request this confirmation by using a printed form available from a Social Security office. You may request this form by telephone or in person.

When applying for benefits, a copy of the last federal income tax you filed will ensure that accurate earnings have been considered in the determination of available benefits.

VETERAN'S ADMINISTRATION

Every qualified veteran is entitled to a lump sum benefit to defray funeral and burial expenses. In addition, there may be an additional allowance for a burial plot in a private cemetery. Other available benefits include an American flag for the casket and a suitable bronze or granite memorial tablet or marker. A surviving spouse is eligible for an adjacent burial plot at a National cemetery subject to space limitations.

Claims for benefits may be filed either by a survivor, a non-relative with proof of funeral service payment, or the funeral director may be authorized by the family to file the claim. All claims must be made on authorized forms from the V.A. Often these may be obtained from the funeral director. Documents necessary to file a claim include:

(1) Veteran's discharge papers.

(2) Certified copy of the death certificate.

(3) Copy of the marriage certificate (if applicable).

(4) Birth certificates of minor children.

(5) Receipted itemized bill from the funeral home.

There may be other benefits also, such as Group Life Insurance, Educational Assistance for Dependents, Counseling, etc. Send for "A Summary of V.A. Benefits" pamphlet from the Veterans Administration, Washington, D.C. 21420. This should provide information on benefits, a list of V.A. offices, and the insurance centers that are closest to you. For the V.A. office closest to you, you may also contact the Federal Information Center.

MILITARY

Upon the death of active and retired members of the military, their survivors are usually entitled to benefits. These may include insurance, household goods storage/ movement, and relocation of dependents, medical care and a survivor benefit plan. If you or your spouse were on active duty, contact the nearest branch of Service for specific information. If you do not already have a contact address, consult your local telephone directory under the Federal Government listings for the branch of service.

CIVIL SERVICE

If you are eligible for any Civil Service benefits, you will need to apply for benefits. There are residual or lump sum payments or annuity benefits. These are determined by length of service. If you are unable to contact a local agency, you may file with the Civil Service Bureau of Retirement Insurance and Occupational Health (Civil Service Commission), 1900 E Street N. W., Washington, D. C. 20415. If you are not sure of the closest agency to contact, call your nearest Federal Information Center.

INSURANCE/ANNUITIES

A claim for payment on a life insurance policy is usually quite simple. A claim form accompanied by a certified copy of the death certificate will suffice. Some of the information required on a claim form will be the policy number, full name and address of the deceased, and possibly the date and place of birth. If there are difficult questions or unknown answers, you may contact a local agent or the Home Office for assistance. If you have contacted someone to obtain your claim form, note the name of the person and the telephone number, so it will be easier if you need to contact them again for further assistance.

The claim form must be completed to collect funds. The claimant should request an optional payment plan if a single-sum settlement is not desired. It may be advantageous to withdraw some funds for immediate needs, and make arrangements to delay further payment of funds. Find out if you can receive life income or fixed installments and how long you can delay the final decision. This gives you the opportunity to consult with advisors and decide what your needs will be when you are more settled. Life Insurance proceeds are not a part of the decedent's probate estate, and are not included in probate. If the claim is to be paid to an estate, the administrator or executor will need to complete the claim form.

Be careful not to overlook old insurance policies. There may still be benefits to be paid on lapsed policies, or you may have located a paid-up policy. Some old policies may even have interest due, so be sure to submit any you find. Also, do not overlook the possiblity that the deceased may have been involved in some insurance benefits through membership in organizations or clubs. These inquiries may bring welcome and unexpected funds. If you suspect there may be life insurance policies that you haven't located, you may write to the American Council of Life Insurance (ACLI). The address is ACLI, Policy Search, 1001 Pennsylvania Avenue, N.W., Washington, D.C. 20004. Include a self-addressed, stamped envelope, and request that member companies search for a policy under the name of the deceased (or give any aliases you know exist).

If a beneficiary is deceased, his/her beneficiaries may be eligible for the proceeds of the policy. This is another example of why it is vital to complete as many blanks as possible in the Working Guide section of this book. If there is no claim, the insurance money could be paid to the State Treasury of the deceased's home state. Policies should be updated to reflect any changes. You may need to obtain legal advice re insurance title and/or insurance ownership.

Annuities are similar to insurance policies. The difference

between them is that annuities provide tax deferred benefits during the annuitant's lifetime, and the payment can be varied. There are many forms of annuities. Some use funds to invest as well as provide retirement and/or death benefits.

Inquire about credit life insurance if there are credit accounts, i.e., Visa, Mastercard, or mortgages. If credit life insurance exists, it will pay off all unpaid balances. As in other sections of this book, we **urge** you to ASK QUESTIONS! This is the best, and sometimes only, way to learn what you need to know.

A last word. You may want to take a second look at Liability Insurance (sometimes called an Umbrella Policy). This is not costly, yet gives coverage for all liability above and beyond that which is covered in other insurance policies. This insurance provides you with security under the worst circumstances, and safeguards home, vehicles, businesses, investments, as well as situations that may have legal consequences.

FINANCIAL MATTERS

CHECKING ACCOUNTS

Most people have at least one checking account. If you need to locate an established account, cancelled checks and/or a savings passbook may provide this information.

If someone is ill or living alone, it is a good time to consider establishing a joint checking account. Some considerations for selection of a checking account follow.

There are a variety of alternatives in choosing a checking account that best meets the need at the lowest total cost. Three basic considerations are cost, convenience and courtesy. Since all banks do not charge in the same way, your analysis of cost should take the following into account.

- Is there a requirement for a minimum balance?
- How many checks may be written each month?
- How is the balance calculated, i.e., average, daily, or lowest balance?
- Is there a monthly maintenance fee?
- What are the charges for bounced checks (yours or others written to you)?
- Is there a charge for a stop-payment order?
- Is there a charge for blank checks?
- Does the use of automated checking incur a charge?
- Are the cancelled checks returned without a charge?
- Is there a charge for duplication of cancelled checks?

To analyze convenience, you may consider:

- ➢ Is it necessary to drive across town to bank?
- ➢ If you use an out-of-state account, will you be able to cash a check when you need it ?
- ➢ Are there automated tellers that are conveniently located, and well lighted for night banking?
- ➢ A thought about courtesy...you may need personal attention for the account. What type of service is offered?

AUTOMATION IN CHECKING ACCOUNTS

In addition to automatic tellers which dispense cash, automation may be used to transfer funds between accounts, pay bills such as home loans, and accept deposits. Direct deposits may be received from federal and/or employer sources. Computer terminals at many retail stores allow speedy verfication of the customer's credit at time of purchase or may automatically debit the amount of purchase from the account.

CHECKING ACCOUNTS AS A RESOURCE TOOL

If you are unaware of the deceased's assets and liabilities, the checkbook, bank statements and file of cancelled checks can give you reliable information about the individual's activities. In addition, it may give you information about future assets by looking at the source of deposits, e.g., rentals, dividends, payments on loans owed to the deceased, insurance dividends, retirement benefits, etc.

SAVINGS ACCOUNTS and C.D.'S

Savings accounts are available at credit unions, commercial banks, mutual savings banks, savings and loan associations and through brokerage houses. Usually, they are passbook accounts or savings certificates of deposit which are commonly called C.D.'s.

The passbook savings account is an "open-end" agreement between the customer and the institution in which the customer may deposit funds or withdraw funds at any given time. The passbook account customer usually receives a small booklet or passbook in which each deposit and/or withdrawal is noted. Interest on the account is added to the customer's balance. Interest rates vary with the institution, and the rates are set forth in the rules and regulations of the passbook account. The Federal Deposit Insurance Corporation (FDIC) offers insurance of $100,000 per account for all savings and checking accounts in commercial and mutual savings banks. In Savings and Loan Association banks, the insurance agency is the Federal Savings and Loan Insurance Corporation (FSLIC) or an extension of the FDIC, while federally insured credit unions are insured under the National Credit Union Administratlon (NCUA). To qualify for the $100,000 insurance, each account must have a different name, e.g., Mr. & Mrs. Dough, Mr. Dough and Mrs. Dough, for a total of $300,000. If there is more in the account in the same name, only $100,000 is insured by the Federal Government. Other institutions may also offer insurance. If so, they must post this information in a prominent place. The rate of interest on savings accounts is often lower than other investments.

The C.D. is a contractual agreement between customer and institution in which there is a specified fixed period of time for the deposit. C.D.'s usually pay a higher rate of interest than passbook accounts. It pays to "shop around" for the best interest rate and to make sure your money is protected through insurance. The minimum investment for a C.D. is typically $500 or $1000. If you withdraw a C.D. early and interest rates have risen since the C.D. was issued, the C.D. will be worth less. If interest rates have dropped, your C.D. will have greater value with early withdrawal and reinvestment. Some considerations for selection of savings accounts and C.D.'s are:

$ Yield - Savings accounts and C.D.'s have traditionally provided the lowest yields in investment vehicles. To determine the <u>true</u> yield, check the annual interest rate payable, as well as the frequency of compounding and crediting interest. Since rates may vary over time, it is wise to find out HOW changes in interest are communicated to the public.

$ Liquidity - Savings from passbook accounts may be withdrawn anytime. This gives them high liquidity. C.D.'s have specific time frames, e.g., 6 months to 5 years so that penalties are applied for early withdrawal. If interest is <u>not</u> credited daily to passbook accounts, some interest will be lost if withdrawal is made prior to the end of a calendar quarter.

$ Safety - Accounts insured by the Federal Government have the highest degree of safety.

$ Hedge Value - Inflation or rising prices may <u>decrease</u> the value of funds held in savings accounts or C.D.'s.

$ Pledge Value - You can usually <u>borrow</u> up to 90% of the total amount in your account with presentation of your passbook to a loan officer of the institution.

$ Taxes - Historically, interest on savings accounts and C.D.'s have been taxable for federal and most state income taxes.

☞ *To avoid unpleasant surprises about the balance in your accounts, it is wise to check the requirements for account activity. Some institutions may deduct a monthly fee or the account may be considered dormant and assets transferred to the State.*

FINANCIAL GUIDANCE

Just about everyone will need financial guidance when faced with settling an estate or preparing to settle an estate. In addition to normal taxes there may be unusual circumstances that require professional services.

It is important to compile complete and orderly information to obtain the most favorable outcome for you . Ask questions, so that you can learn how your input will bring the greatest benefits.

Acquaintances will be a good resource for referrals. Look for someone who has had to deal with similar circumstances. When you make inquiries, you will find that your situation is not unusual, and as an added benefit, it is a way others can help you.

When dealing with a professional, ask for a conference (either on the telephone or in person). Ask questions so that you can make an effective decision . Remember, you pay the bills for this service. You are entitled to competent service, as well as reasonable rates and a comfort level when dealing with the person(s) providing the service.

When dealing with taxes, you can attempt to do-it-yourself, seek preparation assistance from the IRS (if you qualify) or seek private assistance. There are several catagories of individuals who do tax preparation and planning. To determine the level of expertise you will need is not easy. If you have businesses, rental property and/or investments, you should consider a CPA who specializes in taxation or an Enrolled Agent (EA). For more complex returns, consider a tax attorney. Fees will vary with the experience, expertise, and training of the professional.

In addition to tax preparation, some CPA's and EA's also analyze financial projections, conduct feasibility studies for business plans, and assess the impact of mergers and acquisitions. CPA's and EA's may also be qualified Financial Planners, capable of acting as a broker in the purchase or sale of securities. (Please refer to the section on Financial Planners, p. 61.)

Not as well known as CPA's are Enrolled Agents (EA). Like some CPA's, an EA is a tax professional. An EA has demonstrated competence and professional ethics to the Treasury Department and has been granted the privilege to represent clients before the Internal Revenue Service. In addition to Enrolled Agents, state licensed certified public accountants (CPA's), and attorneys are the three categories who may represent all taxpayers before the IRS. If you are not satisfied with the service provided by these professionals, contact the IRS for an EA, the State Bar for an attorney, or the State Licensing Agency for a CPA. Public accountants should not be confused with CPA's. CPA's must pass extensive exams to be certified. A public accountant can be of service to individuals or small businesses that have simple accounting needs.

There are requirements that professional tax preparers must fulfill for each client.

$ The preparer must sign and include his/her Social Security number or employer's tax ID number on each prepared return.

$ The taxpayer must be given a copy of the return when the original return is presented for signature.

$ The professional preparer must retain a copy of all returns they have prepared for three years after the tax year in question, for the purpose of government inspection.

$ Professional preparers cannot negotiate refund checks for taxpayers to pay preparation fees.

National and local tax services exist that can prepare simple returns that do not justify the expense of a CPA. The level of competency will vary a great deal and requires a great deal of scrutiny and/or personal referrals.

Although the preparer must also sign your tax returns, **you** are the one the IRS will ultimately hold responsible for the correctness and completeness of the return. Your preparer will interecede in your behalf with the IRS, but if there is an error, the IRS collects unpaid taxes and penalties, plus interest from you.

FINANCIAL PLANNERS

Many individuals call themselves financial planners. They may or may not meet your needs. Some assurance may be gained if the person meets the standards of the Registry of Financial Planning Practitioners that has been established by the International Association for Financial Planning. Financial planning may be done by a Certified Financial Planner (CFP). Others may include a lawyer or Certified Public Accountant (CPA).

The planner should be capable of working with legal documents and be familiar with retirement plans, estate planning, wills, trusts and tax-advantaged investments. The planner works with other professionals, e.g.,the accountant or lawyer with whom you already may have a professional relationship. The basic process of financial planning includes:

1. Clarifying your present financial situation via collection and assessment of all relevant data, e.g.,wills, insurance policies, tax returns, employee benefits, property, income, indebtedness, and expenses.
2. Identification of personal and financial goals.

3. Identification of barriers to your goals, e.g., inappropriate insurance and/or investments .

4. A written plan with recommendations.

5. Suggestions to carry out the recommendations through the planner or other specialists.

6. Periodic review and revisions of the financial plan.

If you decide to use a financial planner, ask for an interview to become familiar with the following:

a. The planner's background, education and experience.

b. References - clients who accept inquiries.

c. Competence in various types of investments, e.g., tax-advantaged vehicles, insurance, and tax strategies.

d. Working procedures and use of staff.

e. Fees.

f. Existence of a newsletter to communicate with clients.

g. Registration with the SEC and state.

There are three basic payment methods. In Fee Only, the planner bills on a flat or hourly rate. In Fee and Commission, there is a flat fee plus commission on investment products that you purchase. A third method is Commission Only, where the only compensation is commissions on the investment products that you purchase.

The payment method should be discussed, and you should be satisfied with the method you choose. With any investment purchase, you will need to investigate your risk.

BROKERS/BROKERAGE FIRMS

A registered representative, known as a "Stockbroker" is someone who acts on a customer's behalf as an agent in the purchase or sale of investments. He/she is compensated by a "brokerage commission" which is charged each time a stock is bought or sold. Trust is a necessary ingredient when selecting and dealing with a broker. Your financial well-being depends on the expertise and integrity of the broker. Also, you will want to evaluate the reputation of the Brokerage firm that employs him/her.

In selecting a broker, consider an interview, just as you would with a prospective attorney or CPA. One reason is the obvious need to trust the professional ability of the broker, and the other is that your broker may have to work with your attorney and/or accountant on some future matters.

Be sure to ask about all of the services available to you through the brokerage firm. These can be varied and vast. You will want to be sure the firm has membership in all of the stock exchanges; and provides service for mutual funds, pension funds, stocks and bonds, etc.

An interview will probably be hectic because of the nature of the job environment, but ask if the stockbroker is a graduate of an extensive training course and has passed a comprehensive test prepared by the New York Stock Exchange and the National Associations of Securities Dealers. Consider your comfort level with the broker, his/her investment philosophy, commission rates, and the firm's research quality. If the broker has hundreds of clients, will your account be a low priority and therefore be overlooked or handled by an assistant?

If your dealings with the broker take place because you are acting as an executor or to fulfill power of attorney duties, you may need to ask for assistance regarding proxy cards, transfer of ownership on investments, or effects of stock held in "street name".

When securities are held in the "street name", they are held in the name of the broker rather than in the name of the customer. This is sometimes done for convenience, but it may affect the liquidation or transfer of securities in the case of a death, or long illness. Discuss the ramifications with your broker.

Look for professional assistance to help you decide whether to sell, trade, or retain investments. You will need to consider the laws of the State, and who owns the securities.

Usually, there is no great rush to make these decisions. If you are unsure or uncomfortable, don't rush and DO seek assistance.

CONSUMER CREDIT

Can You Get Credit?

Most of us have borrowed money through the use of credit. We applied for it, and our ability to repay was verified to charge purchases, finance a home, auto, boat, etc., and/or received the cash needed for our debts or future goals. Obtaining credit usually requires an assessment of the three C's: capacity, character, and collateral .

- $ Capacity asks the question, "How much can the borrower handle with their present income and expenses?"

- $ Character examines the borrower's past record. How often has the person borrowed? Have deadlines for repayment been met?

- $ Collateral is a lender's insurance policy. If the borrower does not repay the loan, how can the lender collect via the borrower's savings, investments, property, etc.?

Most communities have credit bureaus. These bureaus gather information on the credit performance of individuals in that community. Federal laws control what credit bureaus do and your rights concerning your credit history. You may get your credit rating through payment of a minimal fee to a credit bureau. The name and address of your credit bureau may be obtained from a creditor. A lender usually contacts a credit bureau to obtain a current credit profile and assess risk. This report also provides a guide for the amount of credit that will be given. Your good credit history is a valuable asset which should be carefully guarded!

While we are grieving, there often is a period of disorganization when we are less cautious and are anxious about financial matters. Often there is no urgency to make immediate changes. Do give yourself time and seek out reliable sources of assistance so that you will safeguard your assets and credit history.

Types Of Credit

There are two types of credit between lender and borrower: open-ended and installment credit.

$ Open-ended credit is the term used for charge accounts and credit cards. Once qualified, you agree to pay for all items purchased on credit within a certain number of days. There may be a limit to the charges that may be applied on a specific account. Federal law requires the lender to disclose the method of determining the finance balance as well as the period of time that may elapse before finance charges are applied. The lender must also disclose any annual fee for their services of bookkeeping, billing, etc.

$ Installment credit is the term used for a debt which is repaid in two or more payments made at regular intervals over a period of time. It is often used for the purchase of higher priced items such as appliances or cars. The items purchased may be used as collateral. Installment credit usually requires a down payment, immediate interest charges, a rigid repayment schedule, and may include a prepayment penalty. Installment credit includes a purchase agreement written by a creditor, a bank, or major finance company. (These agreements may be sold in a "market" to other buyers.) The purchase agreement may include a sales contract with details of the sale; a note specifying the amount of payments; repayment schedule and default agreement; and/or credit, life, disability or specified type of insurance.

CONSIDERATIONS WHEN SHOPPING FOR CREDIT

1. Do you want to use credit for an expensive item or to pay many bills ? What is it for ?

2. What type of credit meets your requirements, e.g., open-ended or installment ?

3. How much will credit cost you ? Do lenders vary ?

4. Can you afford credit? What are your present debts ?

5. What is the repayment schedule ? Longer schedules increase the credit charge.

6. If you had an emergency, would credit charges create a strain on the budget ?

7. What is the reputation of the lender ?

8. Are your credit accounts up-to-date before you apply for credit ?

9. Does the lender have specific requirements, e.g.,years on the job, in residence, etc.?

10. Do you know your budgetary limits ? The lender will ask.

11. Is there another person to share your indebtedness, e.g., spouse, family member ?

12. Are you willing to change some of your banking to a new institution if you apply for credit at a new bank ?

13. Is it the right time for a loan? If there is no urgency, will interest rates be more favorable at another time ?

FINANCE CHARGES

Finance charges include interest and "carrying costs", i.e., bookkeeping, credit investigations, allowances for bad debts, credit, life and/or disability insurance, etc. These charges are an important consideration to you and you should be fully aware whether the lender's quote is appropriate or accurate plus the financial cost to you for the use of financing.

In making your decision about finance charges consider the following:

$ What does the credit cost - the Annual Percentage Rate (APR) ?

$ How much interest would you receive in a liquid investment (e.g.,saving account) if you made regular deposits and bought the item for cash at a later date ?

$ What is your best guess about the effect of inflation? Will the cost rise if the purchase is delayed? Will obligated repayment dollars have less purchasing power anyway ?

$ What is the effect upon income taxes? What interest charges are deductible if you itemize ?

The suggestions about consumer credit noted in this section provide some guidelines. They are not meant to be comprehensive. For more in-depth discussion and/or assistance, do consult one or more of the many excellent references you will find in your library or book store. Seek assistance and ask questions of trusted advisors to safeguard your resources and use them wisely.

CREDIT CARDS

Most of us have one or more credit cards. Sometimes they have been issued in a spouse's name, and we may have requested that our name also be on the account so that our own credit has been established. Credit cards are offered by banks, savings and loan institutions, as well as private credit organizations such as American Express, etc. Recently, educational and service organizations have joined with banks to offer cards. Credit cards are honored extensively throughout the U.S. and abroad. When you receive a credit card, a "line of credit" is established. This is the maximum amount that should be charged against the card. One monthly statement is issued for all charges to the account. The card user is expected to pay at least a certain monthly minimum. Unpaid balances are charged interest (finance charges) and charges vary. If debts are paid within a specified time, there is no interest charge. An annual fee is usually charged for the use of the card. It is <u>very</u> easy to lose control of your spending through the use of this convenient form of credit. If you spend only within the limits of a budget, you can maintain control. The credit card allows you to carry less cash and to reduce your expenditures through purchase of sale items. The key word is <u>responsible</u> use of credit - prompt payment to avoid interest charges and a realistic appraisal of your present and future personal goals. How much can you afford? What can you handle with your present income and expenses ? What income is expected in the future?

Some comparisons to consider in the selection of a credit card include:

1. What is the effective cost of the card, i.e., what is the monthly and annual percentage rate for the unpaid balance ? This varies. Often, competitive rates are published in the financial section of your newspaper.

2. What are the conditions of payment ? How many days are provided for payment of the bill without interest charges ? When does interest start accruing ?

3. What is the annual fee?

4. Is the card accepted widely?

5. What is the maximum credit limit?

6. What is the maximum payment period?

7. What is the reputation of the issuing organization?

MEDICAL MATTERS

HOW TO FIND MEDICAL CARE

Most of us have had some experience that will be useful in the selection of medical care. The following summary is written to suggest some questions/answers that can help you to evaluate your present medical arrangements and to suggest some guidelines for the future.

Away From Your Usual Residence:

A. Emergency - Call 911 on the telephone, in the U.S.

B. Non-emergency -

1. Call the local large hospital or medical center for a referral. You will usually receive the names of three doctors.

2. Check with your hotel/motel front desk.

3. Check with family/friends in the area.

At Home:

A. Emergency - Call 911. If you are given an option for hospitalization, select the health care facility where your doctor is on staff.

B. Doctor Selection -

1. If you plan to move, ask your present doctor for a referral.

2. Find your new doctor BEFORE there is a need.

3. Ask your new neighbors about doctors, dentists and pharmacists in your area.

4. Ask for recommendations from someone in the medical field, i.e., a nurse, social worker, etc., who

currently works in health care.

5. Check your telephone yellow pages. (This can be risky.)

6. Check your library for a copy of an American Medical Association Directory of physicians. This reports year of birth, medical school, year licensed to practice, type of practice (general or specialty), active vs. retired, and academic affiliations.

7. Check your local and/or hospital library or the County Medical Association for a specialist who is listed in the Directory of Medical Specialists.

8. Your Social Security office has a listing of doctors who accept Medicare assignment,

9. Set up an appointment; you may be charged for a regular office visit. This will help you make a decision whether you and the doctor can be in a partnership to achieve the best level of health that is possible. It is wise to ask questions on the phone from office personnel. Some appropriate questions are:

❑ Who covers the practice on weekends/vacations?

❑ How are patients seen --- first-come, by appointment? Is there a long wait when you have an appointment?

❑ What are the fees; initial visit, regular visit? What are the charges for office procedures, e.g., X-rays, EKG's?

❑ When does the M.D. bill? Is immediate payment required? Does the office handle insurance claims? Does the practice take Medicare or state medical assistance? Are credit cards accepted?

❐ Does the M.D. recommend vitamins; M.D's thoughts re nutrition, exercise, preventive medicine. Does the M.D. provide formal patient education? How?

After your visit, make a note of your reactions. Are you satisfied?

RATING THE DOCTOR

Some Conditions Are:

❐ Some authorities recommend an M.D. who practices as part of a multi-specialty group.

❐ What hospitals does your M.D. use? How big are they? (Often hospitals with more than 200 beds have more advanced equipment/services.)

❐ What are your M.D.'s credentials? Some of the following are suggested as measures of additional expertise. Does the M.D. have a teaching appointment at a medical school? Is the M.D. Board Certified? (This requires an extensive exam.) Is the M.D. a fellow, i.e., a member of an honorary group with the prestige of peers in the specialty and responsibility for teaching, writing and publishing in medical journals?

❐ Has your M.D. been president or chief of the medical staff in the hospital where the M.D.'s patients are admitted - or involved with the county medical staff? These positions require extra work , show the respect of colleagues and are usually reflected in their practice.

❐ If the M.D. is a family practice physician, the M.D. may be certified by the American Academy of Family Practice. This requires a three year residency and recertification every three years.

❒ How many patients does your M.D. see in one hour? (A typical visit usually lasts about fifteen minutes.)

❒ How many societies does your M.D. belong to? (If your M.D. is listed in the Directory of Medical Specialties, the societies are usually listed.)

❒ What kind of office staff does the M.D. have?

A. Any specialties, e.g., nurse practitioners or physician's assistants?

B. Is the staff friendly ? helpful ?

C. What is the M.D.'s "bedside" manner? Is it acceptable to you? Do you have access to your records? If you go to another community or are travelling, can you carry your own record with you?

The above questions are not exhaustive, but do provide some guidelines for family, friends and care givers as well as the patient.

CONTINUING MEDICAL INSURANCE

You should not assume that you will have continuing medical coverage from the deceased's place of employment. Contact his/her employer to learn what you must do for coverage, the cost of coverage, and the length of time you will qualify. Do some comparison shopping to learn if you can get the same benefits at a better price.

REAL ESTATE HOLDINGS

Any real estate has continuing responsibilities, as well as benefits and pleasures. When considering your home, emotional attachment is another dimension. If you lose a spouse or close family member, your home may become prey to rackets and schemes soon after newspapers publish the news of the death. Be aware and use caution.

Do nothing immediately if it is possible to delay decision making. Take short trips away from your residence, visit a possible future home, and then return to the comfort and safety of your familiar surroundings. If, after several short periods trying out other locations, you decide to liquidate your real property, prepare to do so in the best possible way for you.

If you do not reside alone, a move to a new dwelling will necessitate choices such as the size of your new residence; and location of schools, hospitals, churches, shopping facilities, and public transportation.

If you decide to use a real estate broker for the sale of your residence, shop for services. There may be significant advantages with some brokers. Ask your broker (or agent) to inform you of selections for services such as lenders, title company, etc. Reserve the right to confirm or reject the selections. The broker's basic objective is to obtain a signed contract which properly expresses the agreement of the parties, and to complete the sale. Laws require that the broker be fair in his/her dealings with all parties in the transaction. If you have any questions about being treated unfairly, you should feel free to point this out to the broker before the completion of negotiation. Once you have signed documents, you have essentially agreed to everything as it is, and undoing this can be just about impossible, and very costly.

IMPORTANT: If it is included in Escrow Instructions (or title/deed agreements with conditions to be fulfilled), it is binding to all involved parties!

Some things that are part of the fees and will affect your profit from the sale:

✓ Termite inspection and repairs, if there has been infestation.

✓ How will you receive payment (all financed through an institution or will you be carrying papers)?

✓ Will there be fixtures or appliances left behind that need to be replaced?

✓ Do new owners want fixtures or appliance sites to be repaired or replaced?

✓ Mortgage Insurance (if applicable).

✓ Title Insurance and Title Search (if applicable).

✓ Document Preparation (legal papers, such as Deed of Trust, note, etc.).

✓ Notary Fee (if applicable).

✓ Settlement Charges.

✓ Broker's Fees.

If you decide to handle the sale of property alone, with limited broker service, or an attorney, you must be prepared to be more involved with the sale and the follow up steps required to complete the sale successfully. This can be more time consuming and less effective than engaging a professional who is experienced and reliable. As we have recommended for other situations, request referrals from trusted friends and family.

If you are alone, you may want to consider sharing your home with another, thereby sharing costs, cooking chores, gardening, etc., and gaining companionship. There are referral services available in many cities for those who want shared housing.

The security of your residence is something you may want to investigate, if you have not already done so. Consider alarm systems, first aid self-help (personal radio transmitters, Life Line, etc.), fire extinguishers, earthquake preparedness, etc. If you are a woman living alone, be sure your telephone listing does not indicate this.

If you are faced with the disposal of a family home and the relocation of an elderly relative, there are many considerations. It is important to have people of any age remain as independent as possible. Help them maintain their independence.

Alternative Housing

There is an alternative to selling a family home if it is large enough. Accessory apartments are a means of remaining in the home by forming an apartment for the owner of the home and renting the remaining, larger portion. This way there is no sale of the family home, and the home owner has the benefit of remaining in familiar surroundings, while gaining some added income.

Also, there is ECHO housing (Elder Cottage Housing Opportunity). These are small self-contained, and possibly portable housing, Sometimes these are called "Granny Flats".

Supportive housing has a variety of forms. These include Board and Care as well as Congregate Housing (daily activities with others plus private living quarters with a kitchen for light meals). Continuing Care Communities are independent living arrangements with affiliate nursing facilities.

If you elect to remain in your own home, but need assistance, you can employ skilled nurses, nurse's aides, or a live-in companion . Be very sure you acquire help that is bonded and can provide proof of bonding. Also, ask for references and actually contact some references before allowing someone to move into your home. There are too many consequences that can be impossible to correct after a hasty decision. If you determine the selection is a mistake, do not hesitate to correct the situation with a prompt dismissal. This is one of those times you need to rely on your instinct and act upon it.

And finally, there is the Nursing Home for those who are unable to be independent. These provide caretaker services for daily needs, plus medical care .

Your choice will depend on financial ability, the health of the individual, what is available in the area you select, as well as many other variables . Remember, to seek information from county and federal agencies. Some religious affiliations may offer facilities. Your local hospital, county and/or city social service departments have a great variety of information that can provide resources for many services. Just remember that you will get the assistance you need if you ask the right questions of the right person, so...

KEEP ASKING QUESTIONS!!

CHOOSING A LAW FIRM

If you do not already have a lawyer, you may need to select one to provide services or advice. To find a lawyer, you can seek referrals from acquaintances, friends and relatives, but be sure you value the opinion of the person making the referral. You may also contact your local Bar Association.

Some lawyers advertise in the newspaper and yellow pages of your telephone directory. This may not be the best way to obtain legal services, but it does give a name to investigate.

Your public library should have the Martindale-Hubbell Law Directory. This publication is over 100 years old, and contains the names of members of the bar in the United States and Canada. You will find brief biographical sketches of many lawyers and legal areas in which law firms practice.

Names can be obtained from Lawyer Referral services, but it has been suggested that these names rotate to give lawyers equal opportunities for referrals. This may be useful for the lawyers, but does not necessarily provide you with the most competent lawyer for your particular needs.

Important points to consider when selecting an attorney:

- You should feel comfortable with the way the lawyer or associate handles your concerns.
- It is vital that an attorney presents information to you in a manner that you understand.
- Do you feel rushed?
- Ask about the lawyer's legal expertise.
- Are the rates beyond your financial means or unreasonable?
- Does the attorney charge the same rates to read documents and advise as he/she does to be present at a settlement?

If you are experiencing discomfort, keep looking. There is someone else who can serve your legal needs, and make the process palatable for you.

It is possible to have more than one attorney serve your legal needs. Some situations require that an attorney specialize. If an attorney is not qualified to deal with your situation and give you the best representation, engage an attorney with special knowledge for that type of legal matter. Your general practice attorney may fill generalized needs, but will be more costly due to many extra hours of research. Attorneys who specialize usually give the best representation for specialized and complicated cases.

Arrange for a first conference, and ask specific questions. Look for clear, concise answers. You should feel that the lawyer in question is talking to you, NOT down to you. Ask hourly fees for the lawyer and legal assistants.

Remember, the more information you provide, the less unnecessary time will be required to prepare your case. This way, you are an informed participant that can eliminate unneeded research by a law firm and aid in a successful financial and legal outcome.

After you have selected an attorney, some suggestions that will help smooth the process:

- Ask your lawyer to keep you informed about the progress of your case.

- Request copies of ALL letters and documents that are prepared on your behalf.

- Be sure you fully understand anything that you must sign BEFORE you sign it! Ask what the significance is of the document. Be persistent if you do not receive informed answers .

- If you have an attorney represent your interests in a real estate transaction, your interests may not be fully represented if he/she is acting as a closing agent. The attorney is required to represent all parties in the role of closing agent.

As with all of your life experiences, trust your instincts to give you direction. When you learn to trust this "inner voice", you will be less influenced by others who may be marching to a "different drummer".

WILLS

Most people find it difficult to make a last will and testament. They may feel that a will may hasten their demise or just not want to think about it. However, a will is one of the most important actions during your lifetime. It provides a legal document that gives direction for the distribution of the assets you have worked and saved for throughout your life. If minor children are involved, a will directs your wishes for permanent guardianship. You have the opportunity to remember those individuals and institutions that are most important to you. Before writing a will, discuss your concerns with the people who are dear to you. Determine what you want to accomplish with your will.

If you do not have a legal will, the laws of your state will determine the disposal of your property. This may be acceptable to you, but it often does not represent your wishes. Some additional purposes of a will are as vehicles for the economical, efficient disposal of your property and conservation of your assets. A will can be used to designate your choice of an Executor/Administrator and to create trusts. Check with the laws of your state whether the original should be kept by you or your attorney.

Do you need a lawyer to make a will? Although handwritten wills may be valid, they are usually not a good substitute. A will should be correct technically and should accurately spell out your desires. Each state has specific laws governing estates. The lawyer you choose should know the laws concerning wills and property and be familiar with State and Federal death taxes. A prudent person should update a will every three years. Circumstances may dictate the need to amend or change a will . Some life changes that may prompt a change include:

- Moving to a new state with new laws that have a slight or significant impact upon an estate plan.
- Changes in family circumstances or your desires about distribution of your assets.
- Changes in your assets and liabilities.
- Death of an heir, executor or administrator. If the named executor has become incapable, you will wish to change Executor/Administrator.
- Major changes in tax laws.

EXECUTOR/ADMINISTRATOR/PERSONAL REPRESENTATIVE (INTERCHANGEABLE USE)

An Executor is a person or institution named in a will who has the responsibility to handle the affairs of an estate. The Executor is granted broad powers in carrying out your wishes. Thus, the Executor should be trustworthy, responsible, and capable of administering the matters that may be associated with a probate process or more personal matters of your family. If you are not sure how capable a relative or friend might be even with the assistance of a lawyer and/or accountant, you might consider a professional trust company. They will be impersonal but will charge fees. Some people try the alternative of appointing a close friend or relative and a professional trust company as Co-Executors. Some choose to require the Executor to be bonded. An Executor may be paid a fee for the administrative duties or may waive the right to fees.

PROBATE

Unless a trust agreement, previous disposition of assets by gift, or joint ownership is in effect, the probate process may need to be carried out. This is a court proceeding in which the validity of your will is established and the Executor is empowered to carry out your wishes unless the will has been contested. The laws and fees associated with probate differ from state to state. The executor, with guidance from an attorney and/or accountant,will be responsible for a careful accounting to the court for the administration of the estate. The process can be time consuming and will involve fees. Individual state law describes the priority for distribution of an estate. A common order of priority is widow's allowance; funeral expenses; expenses of a final illness; estate and other taxes due to the federal government, state, and city; legal debts; and finally survivors' bequests.

TRUSTS

Trusts may be used in place of or in addition to a will to bequeath or pass assets to heirs or charities. A trust is a legal contract which has "strings attached", and is used for the management and control of assets. It spells out the trustee's powers and responsibilities. A trust may eliminate the requirement for a lengthy, frequently costly, probate process and may lawfully reduce taxes. A trust also provides privacy since the public probate process is avoided.

Trust law is complicated, and a trust should be created with the advice of an attorney. Trusts may be revokable (i.e., withdrawn) or irrevokable (i.e.,permanent). The fee to develop a trust varies with geographic area, size of estate, etc.

There is also paper work involved. All assets must be transferred into the name of the trust. Under a trust, the trustee is the person or firm who has the responsibility to carry out the directions of the trust. A trustee is expected to preserve the principal (or assets) and invest it so that the beneficiaries receive a reasonable return. In addition, there is a responsibility to carry out the wishes of the individual(s) who created the trust in an honest, diligent, and impartial manner. A trustee should be chosen carefully.

You can select individuals (relatives, friends, or associates) or professional trust companies. There are advantages and disadvantages to either choice. A personal choice may not be as capable or may squander your financial resources. A professional trust company will be more impersonal but will charge fees that will affect the trust fund. The trust company may be more permanent.

A trust agreement should be as flexible as possible to allow the trustee to respond to current economic and business conditions as well as changing statutes that govern trust administration. In addition, you should also consider a power of appointment if you create a trust. This is a legal means which allows a surviving beneficiary to identify how income and/or proceeds from the trust will be distributed at their death. This is a protective device for beneficiaries such as unborn grandchildren.

As noted earlier, a lawyer's advice is crucial. The lawyer should be competent in this specialty and be able to answer any concerns you may have about the creation of a trust. If you read and research the topic of trusts before your visit, you will be better prepared to ask the important questions.

DURABLE POWER OF ATTORNEY

This is a legal document providing written authorization from a person giving another person the power to perform binding legal acts on his or her behalf. Obviously, it is a very serious matter and great thought should be given to selection of an individual who can act in your name. It is a very practical document when a person becomes increasingly incapacitated due to an illness (such as Alzheimer's Disease), and is unable or lacks the energy to carry on their own affairs. It is simple to create in consultation with a lawyer. If a conservator/guardian is needed, consult an attorney.

The Durable Power of Attorney ceases upon the death of the individual who provided the authorization.

LIVING WILL

A living will is a document which is available in many states. It authorizes others and/or physicians to make medical decisions for you if you are incapacitated.

The living will is fairly simple and straight forward. Most states require that at least two people (preferably not members of your family) witness the signing of the living will. Some states require that it be notarized. If used, copies should be given to your physician(s), clergy, lawyer, and anyone you have given the power of attorney. There <u>are</u> some states that do <u>not</u> recognize the living will as binding upon physicians. A living will can be revoked by you at any time—usually with an oral statement.

DURABLE POWER OF ATTORNEY FOR HEALTH CARE

This is considered a valuable document to avoid unwanted, prolonged life support situations. The durable power of attorney is more flexible than a living will. It allows you to spell out in detail your precise wishes concerning treatment. In it, you appoint an individual and one or more successive persons to act as primary agent(s) to represent your wishes.

It is important to pick someone you have confidence in and to make sure that person understands your wishes. Ongoing discussion about your wishes is prudent. It is a document every one should execute while they are in good health. In some states, it is valid for seven years. At the end of this time, it is still valid if you are unable due to poor health to renew it.

The document must be witnessed by at least two people who will not benefit by your death, and some authorities recommend that it be notarized. You may also revoke it. Consult the Patient Advocate in your local hospital for a copy or an organization such as Concern for the Dying 250 W. 57th St. N.Y., N.Y. 10107. They can provide more information about your state's laws concerning the Durable Power of Attorney for Health Care. Forms are also available at many local stationery stores, or you may check with your physician.

SAFE DEPOSIT BOX

Many people keep vital documents in a safe deposit box. If you are unaware of the location of the box or key and need to examine the contents, some ideas that may help you are:

A. Locating A Safe Deposit Box- Think about the owner's habits...organized? disorganized? Try desk drawers, etc. You are looking for a flat key. It may have a number imprinted on it and it may be in a small envelope.

Another clue to box location may be found in cancelled checks. Although some banks provide free safe deposit boxes as a benefit for customers with checking/savings accounts, there may be a cancelled check for rental of a safe deposit box. Or, you may wish to contact that particular bank.

If you still have not located the box, you may want to check with other local banks. Banks often require a letter from the probate court giving you permission to examine the contents of a box. You can also write to the American Safe Deposit Association at 330 W. Main Street, Greenwood, Indiana 46142. They have 4000 members and list the names of box owners. There is a fee for this service.

B. Examining The Contents - If you are denied access to the box, you may ask a bank officer to request a State Treasury Representative to make a list of the contents. This can protect you in case there are disputes among beneficiaries. It is a good idea not to open the box unaccompanied if there are additional survivors with interest in the estate. If several beneficiaries are available, have them accompany you and help inventory the contents. Each of the people involved should sign the inventory sheet(s).

If you are the owner of the safe deposit box, we recommend that you list the contents. The Working Guide in this book will help simplify that task. A general rule is to use the box for the safekeeping of irreplaceable items or those which would be costly or troublesome to replace. Most authorities agree that the following should be kept in a safe deposit box:

(1) family birth and death certificates; marriage, divorce and/or separation papers; service and/or veteran's papers and any other document that is either government or court recorded. (If you wish to obtain certified copies of birth, death, marriage and divorce certificates, you may write to the Consumer Information Center, P. O. Box 100, Pueblo, CO 81002 for the booklet WHERE TO WRITE FOR VITAL RECORDS. There will be a smal l fee.)

(2) Copy of a will (the original is often kept by the attorney and another may be kept at home); investment certificates held in your name, e.g., bonds, treasury bills, stocks, C.D.'s; important contracts such as deeds for real estate, automobile titles, leases, notes, and special papers such as patents and copyrights.

(3) Houshold inventory.

(4) (Optional) cash, collectibles, jewelry.

MAIL

If you become responsible for the deceased's mail, it must be monitored regularly (preferably for a year) to make sure that ongoing bills are paid. The mail is also an important source of information, e.g.,bills owed, notices about charge accounts, insurance premiums, other liabilities, as well as dividend and pension checks, bank and/or brokerage statements, etc.

Postal regulations state that in the event of a death, mail may be held for fifteen days before it is returned to the sender. However, most mail can be claimed at the post office or re-addressed through the usual change of address form if an heir can provide proper identification and a copy of the death certificate or letter of authority showing appointment as a personal representative by Probate Court.

All mail is not handled this way. Most U.S.Treasury checks, e.g.,Social Security, V.A. and military pensions must be returned by the postmaster. If you receive one, keep it UNOPENED until notified that the paperwork has been completed, and you are requested to return the check. Other state, county or municipal checks must be handled according to the instructions on the envelope for undeliverable mail. This also applies to documents and mail intended for the sole use of the deceased such as driver's licenses and credit cards.

If you receive something by mail that was not ordered; by law, you are not obligated to return it. If the sender attempts to bill you, ask for proof that the order was placed. If something was ordered by mail and it does not meet expectations, you may wish to write a letter of complaint. A sample letter to contest billing is found on page 125.

The above is the ideal. You may find that mail delivery is uninterrupted. If so, do keep in mind the requirements for return of government checks, etc.

Mail should be monitored for a year since some statements are semi-annual. In other cases, e.g., Certificates of Deposit, insurance policies, the notice may be annual.

POST OFFICE BOX

If a box has been rented,a survivor with a key may continue to collect all mail, but is obligated legally to return U.S. Treasury checks, and items noted earlier. If the survivor does not live at the same residence, it is often more convenient to request a change of address form. Mail can be directed to a surviving spouse, the personal representative appointed by Probate, or to a party designated by family members.

If you suspect there is a post office box, you may have to be creative in finding the key.

You should sort out the mail. If there are joint owners, send or keep the mail for the survivor. The remaining mail can be sorted into assets (checks), liabilities (bills), social correspondence, magazine subscriptions, and advertising. Magazine subscriptions can be transferred or terminated (with a request for a refund on the remaining subscription).

FINAL ARRANGEMENTS

Planning for your funeral while still alive may seem impossible, depressing and maudlin. Yet, this planning shows your concern for your loved ones and demonstrates your wishes concerning your life. Your decisions will provide support and comfort to those who are near and dear to you.

Because there is no "good" time to make funeral arrangements, it is helpful to involve your relatives and/or friends to let them know your wishes. They may respond with a denial about the possibility of death, a "let's not talk about that", but do persevere. IT IS IMPORTANT. At the very least, leave written instructions so that your wishes are known. Although there is no legal obligation to follow these instructions, most survivors will be grateful.

At the death of a loved one, the ability to concentrate is usually limited. Emotional responses often color the best judgment. Families may be unduly influenced by their concern to do the "right thing". The following are some alternatives that should be considered.

Pre-paid Plans/Arrangements

Should you purchase? Some factors that may influence your decision are:

- Will the funeral home be in business when needed?
- If you change your residence, is a refund available? If no refund is available after a change in residence, what costs will be incurred, e.g., transport of remains, family travel/accommodations costs?
- Can the contract be cancelled, switched to a lower cost program, or applied in another geographic area?
- Is there a penalty for late payments of monthly installments?

- ➠ What is the availability and cost of credit insurance?
- ➠ How much time is granted to survivors for payment if the contract is not fully paid at the time of death?
- ➠ What services are included?
- ➠ Is the contract in agreement with local and state laws?

If you do purchase a plan, a regular review and/or update is prudent.

Memorial Society Membership

Memorial Societies are local consumer-oriented organizations that were developed to help people plan for a simple funeral at a reasonable cost. There is a one-time membership fee and the various societies are non-denominational and non-restricted. The Societies DO NOT provide direct interment or disposition services. The type of society also may vary. It may be a CONTRACT Society that works with a customer and a particular mortuary; a COOPERATING Society that refers members at the time of need to one or more local mortuaries known to offer low-cost funerals and have proven themselves previously; or an ADVISORY Society that provides members with the names and addresses of mortuaries that offer inexpensive funerals and competent service.

DONATION OF BODY OR ORGANS (THE UNIFORM DONOR CARD)

If you decide to donate, the first step is to obtain, fill out, and carry with you a Uniform Donor Card (UDC). A UDC can be obtained from the Living Bank, P.O. Box 6725, Houston TX 77005 or by calling 1 800 528-2971 (24 hour Service). In addition, there are over forty states that provide UDC's for valid driver's license holders. Check whether your state allows you to declare your wishes on your license. If it is not allowed, you may still obtain a UDC from the Living Bank.

Even if your state provides a UDC, you may additionally wish to be registered through the Living Bank, since they are an a national registry and can provide 24 hour verification to inquiries. Inform your relatives, friends, lawyer, doctor and anyone close to you of your intentions.

A sample letter for this purpose is included on page 131.

Autopsy

An autopsy is a post-death examination of the body. It may be required when the cause of death is questionable or when there is no attending physician. It may be of help to the deceased's family if it provides information about risk/ hereditary predispositions, if there is concern about negligence from health-care providers, or if knowledge about the cause of death would advance medical science. Family permission is usually required. An autopsy does not eliminate the choice of an open-casket.

FUNERAL HOMES

Try to get referrals from some objective sources such as friends and/or neighbors who have had need of these services. Your church or synagogue may offer suggestions. A funeral home that cooperates with a local memorial society offers another option. There are many honest, competent and caring funeral directors who can and will be reassuring during this difficult time. Some questions to direct your choice may be:

- What type of service?
- Will there be a religious officiant? (Who?)
- Will there be visitation or calling hours?
- Where will the service be held? (Church, funeral home, elsewhere?)

- ➠ What will be the method of final disposition? (Earth burial, entombment, or other disposition of cremated remains?)

- ➠ What type of casket?

- ➠ What costs/services are involved?
(Some answers re costs are available by phone while a more complete listing is available with an in-person visit.)

The usual fees for services include the following:

- ➠ Professional Services -- response to the initial request for service; conference to determine the desired services; coordination and direction of the funeral services and participants; supervision and attendants at visitation, services, and graveside.

- ➠ Facilities -- Use of the facilities for viewing and/or funeral services.

- ➠ Transportation --Transfer of the remains to the funeral home, hearse, limousine, flower car, other vehicles, and traffic control personnel.

- ➠ Other --Acknowledgement cards, forwarding or receiving remains from another funeral home, cremation, casket or burial container, or grave liner.

Your answers to these questions will direct your selection of a funeral provider, the funeral items you want and are able to afford.

Embalming

In most cases embalming is not necessary unless the body must be transported a long distance, there is a highly contagious disease, or burial will be delayed. The mortuary MUST inform you of the regulations concerning embalming. If you do NOT wish to be embalmed, you should inform all concerned individuals of your wishes, state your wishes in your letter of instruction, locate a funeral home that will cooperate fully, and make advance arrangements if possible.

Obituary

Customs and/or wishes about the obituary are often influenced by local practices. If you have specific wishes about the content, be sure to include the information in your letter of instruction about your funeral. In addition to information about the deceased, the notice often contains information about visitation hours, the service and specifics about condolence wishes, e.g., in lieu of flowers donations to charity.

Usually, the funeral director can and will assist survivors in the preparation of a notice. Many newspapers charge a fee for the obituary. Charges are often dependent upon the length of the notice, and the fee schedule.

You should be aware that an obituary notice may prompt the unscrupulous to take advantage of the publicized time devoted to services to commit a burglary. Sometimes the obituary states only the name of the deceased and the funeral home in order to decrease this risk. It is prudent to have a housesitter during the at-risk times of the visitation and service.

Closed vs. Open Casket

The choice is a VERY personal decision. Some people feel an open casket helps survivors to accept a death as a real and final fact while others find it distressing. In addition, an open-casket increases the funeral costs with the need for embalming, cosmetic preparation and clothing. If you have specific wishes about your preference, be sure to make them known.

Death Certificate

The funeral director can assist with the completion of data for certified death certificates. A knowledgeable person should check the information to ensure that it is complete and accurate. Errors can cause delays and be costly. You will need at least ten copies of the certificate to file claims. Photocopies of the certificates are not accepted in all situations.

Notification of Death

Usually your family is aware of the people that should be notified, i.e., friends, relatives and/or business colleagues who may wish to participate in funeral services. After the funeral, the following may need to be notified: Lawyer and/or Accountant, Life Insurance Agent or Home office, Social Security, Civil Service or Military Organization, Social and/or Professional Organizations, Employer and/or Business Associates, Trust Officer. Each organization should inform the survivor(s) of requirements to collect benefits.

Funeral Rites

If you have special wishes about the ceremony, eulogy, and ritual, it is wise to include this information in your letter of instruction. You might want to include remarks for the service, music, and/or choices for pallbearers, interment service and your wishes concerning the inclusion of flowers or a favored charity.

It is often traditional to have a post-funeral gathering of family and friends. If you have specific wishes for food, drink, music, etc., be sure to include this information in your instructions.

Personal Possessions

In an ideal world, we would dispose of all our possessions by the time of our deaths. Unfortunately, we do not live in an ideal world. At a minimum, it is wise to have your wishes known through your will and letter of instruction about specific bequests you wish to make.

Disposal of possessions after a death is a difficult task. From personal experience, we recommend that this should be undertaken as soon as possible after the funeral. If possible, get family and/or friends involved in the task. There are many deserving charities/thrift shops who will appreciate clothing and/or possessions no longer desired by the family of the deceased.

☞ *Caution should be used in disposing of possessions. There may be valuable collectibles, heirlooms or objects of art. If there is any doubt, seek some professional advice and/or comparison shop through the classified ads in a major newspaper. Allow family and close friends to select a personal rememberance before disposal of possessions.*

Ongoing Concerns

You and your loved ones will be grateful if you keep a regularly updated list of all legal and financial papers and where they may be found. The Working Guide in the beginning of this book will simplify and direct this task.

After the funeral, all bills should be collected and paid as soon as possible. Again, the data in the front of this book can be of great benefit to survivors.

Bereavement/Handling Grief

Bereavement is a stressful time for survivors. A period of time for adjustment plus the "work" of grieving is necessary. Survivors should NOT make any major decisions during the first weeks/months of bereavement. If survivors MUST make major decisions, advice should be sought from trusted advisors.

The person who died would not want their survivors to grieve endlessly. This means there is an obligation to go on living; and take care of themselves physically and emotionally. It is necessary to reach outside themselves to maintain old friends, make new ones and adapt to the changes of life.

Survivors need not feel alone. There are excellent support groups. They are available through local religious, health care, and social organizations. Some funeral directors also can give referrals. Whatever group you decide to try, we have found it useful to attend meetings at least three times before deciding if that group serves your needs. When you are feeling frail, your perceptions may not be as accurate as they would be under normal circumstances.

If home or auto maintenance are new requirements, there are courses available through local schools and auto agencies. They also recommend excellent reference texts. Do not overlook recommendations of friends. They often can provide you with a reliable list of repair persons.

Do be kind to yourself and lean into the pain of grief. It hurts, but growth does occur out of the process. Leaning on another can only be temporary; it does not eliminate the pain, nor help the survivor to get on with life.

THE UN'S -- UNWANTED, UNDESIRABLE, AND OFTEN UNSOLICITED!

Consumer fraud is alive, flourishing and big business! Unsuspecting consumers lose $40 billion or more each year. After a loss, you may be more susceptible to a variety of schemes. It is not unusual for obituaries to stimulate a barrage of offers that are designed to relieve you of your money. Unprincipled people also realize that there may be money available from insurance proceeds.

Survivors who are not skilled in financial matters may be sold unwanted merchandise, services, or may be grossly over-charged. In general, it is wise not to sign a contract for services or merchandise from a stranger without checking with your financial advisors and/or available consumer resources such as the Chamber of Commerce, etc. Do NOT publicize your status as a survivor. Use caution; check with your advisors (attorney, etc.) if you are invited to participate in a get-rich-quick opportunity from strangers, friends, or even relatives. Though sincere, they may be unaware of the intended fraud.

Get opinions from several sources. There is a wealth of information available in most communities through public agencies, the school system, libraries, non-profit institutions, and trustworthy family and friends. Ask at least two firms for written estimates on repairs and maintenance.

If you plan to spend a sizeable amount, e.g., for painting, wall-papering, plumbing, etc., ask for names of referrals you may contact.

There is a federal trade commission rule giving you a "cooling-off" period in which you may change your mind about a contractual agreement. For more information about mail orders, you may contact your local postmaster and/or the Federal Information Center listed in your phone book. For the "cooling-off" rule to apply, the purchase must be made at your home or away from the seller's place of business. It must not be at your invitation, e.g., emergency home repairs, and must cost more than $25. Real estate, insurance, securities and mail/phone orders are not covered under this rule.

Do comparison shopping for new equipment and merchandise. Again, you may use your library and telephone to reduce the amount of time and energy you will need to expend. Weigh advice carefully -- especially if the advisor might have a vested interest in your money. As you seek and listen to advice, you may wish to take notes and compare or analyze the information you receive. This general information is intended to urge you to be cautious -- not paranoid. While you are grieving, you may be more susceptible to appeals. Sometimes, there are fraudulent bills for health care. If this happens, contact your insurer and provide details.

If you receive mail solicitations for a "miracle" health product, you should suspect fraud. It is wise to contact the Food and Drug Administration, Consumer Affairs Office, 5600 Fishers Lane, Rockville MD 20857, the Federal Trade Commission, Bureau of Consumer Protection, Washington, DC 20580, or your local consumer protection office. Though time consuming, it is important to investigate.

Free vacations, travel clubs, and time-share condominiums may be other successful con schemes. For a brochure on avoiding travel problems, contact the American Society of Travel Agents. You may also investigate the consumer protection plans offered by the National Tour Association through their members' nationwide travel firms such as American Express. The plan reimburses consumers up to $100,000 for money that has been deposited for travel/ package plans .

The telephone/credit card order is another potential problem area. Many bogus investment schemes (scams) arise from "boiler rooms", i.e.,offices staffed with dozens of solicitors. Your phone number may have been dialed at random, so do not verify your name or phone number for the caller. If the call is initiated by a computer-generated voice, hang up. Or the scheme may be presented in ads, your mail, or by television. Many victims are older adults with accumulated nest eggs. They may be more susceptible because of their concern about their fixed incomes, and their eagerness to get the highest return on their invesments. In general, use GREAT CARE in providing your credit card number to anyone.

Repair fraud is also big business -- particularly for older adults and/or survivors who are more stressed than usual. In some schemes, unscrupulous people take advantage of a home owner's ignorance about roofs, furnaces, plumbing, or major appliances. Car repair can also be costly. Experts suggest the following:

✆ Ask for recommendations for repairs from friends and neighbors.

✆ Call licensing boards (city, county, state) to see if the repairperson has the required licenses.

✆ If a Better Business Bureau is available, check to see if there are unresolved complaints against the contractor.

✆ Check out references.

✆ Obtain written estimates and guarantees. If available, they are only as good as past performance and length of time in business.

✆ Never pay the full amount until the work is done to your satisfaction.

If you suspect investment fraud, you may consult the following organizations.

- The Commodity Futures Trading Commission
  2033 K St., NW, Washington, D.C. 20581

- The National Futures Association
  200 W. Madison Street, Suite 1600
  Chicago, Illinois 60606

- Securities and Exchange Commission
  Office of Consumer Affairs and Information Services
  450 Fifth Street, NW, Washington, D.C. 20549

- National Association of Securities Dealers
  Surveillance Department
  1735 K Street NW
  Washington, D.C. 20006

- American Arbitration Association
  140 West 51st Street
  New York, N.Y. 10020-1203

If you wish to arbritrate a dispute with a broker, you may consult the National Association of Security Dealers, NASD Financial Center, 33 Whitehall Street, New York, New York 10004,your state securities administrator, attorney general, or a regulated stock exchange.

If you believe high pressure is being applied, experts suggest asking:

? Why was I selected?

? How did you get my name?

? Will you please provide references?

? Will you send written guarantees before I provide my credit card or check?

Be suspicious if it sounds too good to be true. It often is! **Expect to be insulted so that you will feel guilty for refusing the offer. Guilt is a powerful motivator!**

MOVING ON

A Final Word

This book has focused upon the nuts and bolts, the practical details that must be dealt with upon the death of a loved one. The great emotional upheaval is often a primary concern which may color all of your responses. This section tries to address this briefly.

Each person experiences their own perceptions and feelings of loss. It is often a maze of unknowns. Losing the role of wife, husband, son or daughter is devastating. How you handle the loss depends on your individual personality and how you define your needs. These needs include sharing your grief yet retaining your privacy and receiving support from friends, family or others who have also experienced a loss.

Recovery/bereavement is a process that is uneven and individual. How long it will take is an individual matter. The initial period of grief may leave you feeling like a ton of bricks has fallen on you. You may feel that no one understands, hope no one will ask how you are, and may find it difficult to believe there has even been a death. You may resent people who tell you how well you look when you are feeling so awful. It's often difficult to read, to concentrate, and to make decisions. You may be very forgetful. Many people report feeling crazy or mentally impaired. The following suggestions may help:

- Feeling crazy- share your concerns; others who are bereaved will echo their own feelings of craziness and assure you of your sanity. Bereavement and/or support groups can be very helpful. Start a journal; it helps with insomnia and a release of feelings.

- Coming home to an empty house -- change your previous habits. Converse with the t.v. and/or radio; plan an exercise session; rearrange the furniture. Consider a pet.

- Security -- have your home checked. Often your police department can provide you with information about locks, suggestions for deterring burglaries, e.g., timers, elimination of landscape which obstructs views of doors and windows, and the use of a Neighborhood Watch. For someone who lives alone and has a need for a personal emergency system, there are various radio transmitters or phone systems, i.e., Life Line. The AARP can provide a list of these resources, their cost and capabilities. Fire extinguishers and smoke alarms should be included in your security check.

- Mail -- On-going bills should be attended to at least twice a month. Letters and cards of condolence may require a response. Most people find it therapeutic to answer the letters, cards and gifts of flowers and food. The tears you shed may help move you along. If it seems impossible, try to enlist family and friends to assist you.

Support Groups

There are a variety of groups that may be helpful for the terminally ill and their families as well as those who are grieving the loss of a loved one. Their support derives from the religious, psychologic/psychiatric, and organized activities that are dedicated to self-help work. Many of their activities overlap.

- Do seek out those resources that are compatible with your life style. Ask your doctor, hospital sources, and/or church affiliations for their recommendations. Many hospitals have chaplains, pastoral care departments, and social service departments that can be of assistance. The clergy often visit the dying person at home and support the family. Local churches, synagogues, and parishes often offer support groups for the widowed. Patients with terminal illness and their families often can be assisted by groups offered through the American Cancer Society. There are a multitude of local groups. These are frequently listed in the local newspapers.

Our experience has been that it is useful to participate in a group and/or consultation at least three times before deciding if the activity is effective or not. There are usually unexpected benefits from seeking out support activities.

Birthdays, Anniversaries, and Holidays

These days present special problems for the bereaved. They seem to exaggerate the loss and pain associated with grief. We suggest that you plan ahead for these special times. Plan to spend your time with family or friends if this is possible. You may wish to invite friends or family to your home, to a restaurant, etc. to give you that extra emotional support that may be needed. If not feasible, try one of the variety of travel excursions available through commercial enterprises and local community services.

Taking Care of Yourself

During the grief process, you may be less attentive, more easily distracted and more emotional. It is very important to be aware of the need to take care of yourself. The following are especially important now:

- Try to eat a balanced diet with a focus on fresh, unrefined and homemade food. It should include wholesome starchy foods, fruits, and vegetables with a limitation on your intake of high-fat foods, sugary snacks and desserts.

- Exercise regularly, and work exercise into your routine activities, e.g., use the stairs instead of elevators, etc.

- Find safe ways to control stress -- a walk, joining a stress management group, writing, etc.

- Watch out for abuse of mood-changing substances such as alcohol, caffeinated beverages, etc. Tranquilizers or sleeping pills must be prescribed and require caution.

- Continue your regular check-ups, i.e., physical exams, vision, hearing and dental visits.

- See your physician as soon as possible if you note a change in your health, e.g., a lump, skin lesions, digestive problems, excessive thirst or urination, blood in the stool, urine, or sputum. Consider professional assistance if you have symptoms of emotional distress, e.g., prolonged insomnia, depression, anxiety etc.

You may be a bit more accident prone. Do use care in your home. Many accidents occur with throw rugs, improvised ladders, etc. Try to be aware of the risks that do exist in your home and when driving. A recent American Journal of Medicine article noted that persons without support systems were most at risk during the grieving process. This emphasizes the need to maintain or establish a support system at this critical time.

Do not be surprised if you find yourself angry with yourself, the deceased, your family, etc. Anger is not unusual. If you already have good coping skills to deal with anger, you are aware of the need to acknowledge feelings and to deal with the anger constructively. It is beyond the scope of this book to discuss appropriate responses in depth. We have found that it is helpful to acknowledge the anger, be as objective as possible about what's going on, and to use the energy to resolve the problem. It may be that you should pursue professional counseling; exercise may be helpful. Letter-writing, heart-to-heart talks with family members, etc. may be the answer, but DO deal with the feelings of anger. **Unresolved anger may result in depression.**

Children's Needs

Children are sometimes neglected with the energy expended to deal with one's own grief. They, too, have lost a significant person in their lives. It may be their first experience with death. They may have unresolved issues with their parents. They, too, will need to address the grief process.

Children (especially adult children) should NOT be expected to take on responsibilities formerly borne by the deceased. Seek or encourage them to seek out support groups that can be of assistance.

Decisions

- Make as few major decisions as possible. Try not to make a household move for a year. Write down the names of business people you deal with and outline a summary of the discussion/events. Inspect wastebaskets carefully to prevent disposal of valuables. Set up and keep files; records are especially important for tax purposes.

- Don't make any long-term commitments. Do try to plan ahead for each new day.

- If you do not already have one, start a list of repair persons. If you have friends or family with tested and competent referrals, do use this information.

Have hope. The changes in your life are painful. These changes require you to be more flexible than you ever could have anticipated. You will certainly learn a great deal about yourself as you cope and adjust to the journey you will take. A great sense of accomplishment accompanies this journey.

CHECKING ACCOUNTS

Designate joint owners, community property, individual, business, etc.

Name of firm:________________________________

Account #:________________________________

Address:________________________________

Name(s) on account:__________________________

Kind of account:_____________________________

Name of firm:________________________________

Account #:________________________________

Address:________________________________

Name(s) on account:__________________________

Kind of account:_____________________________

Name of firm:________________________________

Account #:________________________________

Address:________________________________

Name(s) on account:__________________________

Kind of account:_____________________________

SAVINGS ACCOUNTS/CERTIFICATES OF DEPOSIT MONEY MARKET ACCOUNTS

(Location of immediately accessible funds)
*Indicate with an * if an IRA, Keogh or Tax-deferred account.*

Name of facility:________________________________

Account #:____________________________________

Address:_____________________________________

Name(s) on account:____________________________

Type of account:________________________________

Location of passbook or certificate:__________________

____

Maturity date (in pencil):__________________________

Special instructions/information:____________________

____

Beneficiary:____________________________________

Name of facility:________________________________

Account #:____________________________________

Address:_____________________________________

Name(s) on account:____________________________

Type of account:________________________________

Location of passbook or certificate:__________________

____

Maturity date (in pencil):__________________________

Special instructions/information:____________________

____

Beneficiary:____________________________________

DOCTORS

Indicate Doctor's specialty after name.

Doctor:________________________________

Address:________________________________

Phone#:________________________________

Doctor:________________________________

Address:________________________________

Phone#:________________________________

Doctor:________________________________

Address:________________________________

Phone#:________________________________

CREDIT CARDS

*Indicate credit/life insurance with *.*

Company:____

Address:____

Phone #:____

Card #:____

Company:____

Address:____

Phone #:____

Card #:____

Company:____

Address:____

Phone #:____

Card #:____

Company:____

Address:____

Phone #:____

Card #:____

LIABILITIES

Debts owed by me (vehicle, personal, business, etc.)

*Indicate credit/life insurance with *.*

Owed to:____

Address:____

Name(s) on loan:__________________________________

Account #:______________________________________

Monthly payment:__________________________________

Location of papers:________________________________

Collateral, if any:_________________________________

Owed to:____

Address:____

Name(s) on loan:__________________________________

Account #:______________________________________

Monthly payment:__________________________________

Location of papers:________________________________

Collateral, if any:_________________________________

Owed to:____

Address:____

Name(s) on loan:__________________________________

Account #:______________________________________

Monthly payment:__________________________________

Location of papers:________________________________

Collateral, if any:_________________________________

ASSETS

Debts owed to me (vehicle, personal, business, etc.)

Debtor:____

Address:____

Description of debt:________________________________

Terms:____

Balance (inpencil):_________________________________

Location of documents:______________________________

Debtor:____

Address:____

Description of debt:________________________________

Terms:____

Balance (in pencil):________________________________

Location of documents:______________________________

Debtor:____

Address:____

Description of debt:________________________________

Terms:____

Balance (in pencil):________________________________

Location of documents:______________________________

Stocks *(currently held)*

Company:____

Name(s) on certificate:______________________________

Number of shares:__________Certificate number(s):_______

____

Purchase date(s) and price(s):__________________________

Location of certificate(s):_____________________________

Held in street name? ❒ yes ❒ no

Company:____

Name(s) on certificate:______________________________

Number of shares:__________Certificate number(s):_______

____

Purchase date(s) and price(s):__________________________

Location of certificate(s):_____________________________

Held in street name? ❒ yes ❒ no

Company:____

Name(s) on certificate:______________________________

Number of shares:__________Certificate number(s):_______

____

Purchase date(s) and price(s):__________________________

Location of certificate(s):_____________________________

Held in street name? ❒ yes ❒ no

Bonds / Notes / Bills *(currently held)*

Issuer:____

Issued to:______________________________________

Maturity date:___________________________________

Location of the certificate:_________________________

Held in street name? ❐ yes ❐ no

Issuer:____

Issued to:______________________________________

Maturity date:___________________________________

Location of the certificate:_________________________

Held in street name? ❐ yes ❐ no

Issuer:____

Issued to:______________________________________

Maturity date:___________________________________

Location of the certificate:_________________________

Held in street name? ❐ yes ❐ no

<u>Other Investments</u> - *US Savings Bonds, government securities, etc . For each of these investment, list amount, to whom issued, issuer and maturity date. List the location of the certificates.*

The following securities are pledged against loans or margined:

____

____

They are held by (names & addresses):____________________

____

____

My broker:______________________Phone #:__________

Address:____

____

Account #:____

List additional broker(s)/brokerage house(s):_____________

____

____

LIFE INSURANCE/ANNUITIES

To collect benefits, a copy of the death certificate should be sent to each company. Additional benefits may be available through group policies i .e. labor unions, fraternal organizations or employer.

Full name of insured:____________________________

Owner of policy:________________________________

Insurance company:______________________________

Amount:________________ Kind of policy:______________

Policy #:__________________ Disability option ❒ yes ❒ no

Beneficiaries:__________________________________

Issue date:__________________ Maturity date:____________

Method of payout (or options):________________________

Full name of insured:____________________________

Owner of policy:________________________________

Insurance company:______________________________

Amount:________________ Kind of policy:______________

Policy #:__________________ Disability option ❒ yes ❒ no

Beneficiaries:__________________________________

Issue date:__________________ Maturity date:____________

Method of payout (or options):________________________

Full name of insured:____________________________

Owner of policy:________________________________

Insurance company:______________________________

Amount:________________ Kind of policy:______________

Policy #:__________________ Disability option ❒ yes ❒ no

Beneficiaries:__________________________________

Issue date:__________________ Maturity date:____________

Method of payout (or options):________________________

OTHER ADDITIONAL ENTRIES

APPENDIX

SAMPLE LETTER TO INSURANCE COMPANY

Date

Name of Insurance Company
Address
City, State, Zip Code

Re: ______________________________, deceased; Date of Death: ______________ Policy No.: ____________________

Dear Sir/Madam,

Enclosed is your claim form completed by the named beneficiary (or decedent's estate or personal representative) on the above policy. Also, enclosed you will find a certified copy of the death certificate.

Please send me any appropriate taxation documents. In addition, please process this claim and forward the proceeds to the beneficiary at the address indicated on the claim form. (Or, please inform me of alternative settlement options available other than a lump sum payment.)

Sincerely,

(Signature)

Your name
Address
City, State, Zip Code

SAMPLE LETTER TO DECEASED'S ORGANIZATION(S)

Date

Organization Name
Address
City, State, Zip Code

Re:____________________________________,deceased;Membership No. (if appropriate) ________________________

Dear Sir/Madam,

This is to inform you that ____________________________ died on (day, month, year). I wish to inquire about any life insurance or medical coverage that may have been acquired through your organization. I will provide any documents that you may require from me as his/her beneficiary.

Thank you for your assistance.

Sincerely,

(Signature)

Your name
Address
City, State, Zip Code

SAMPLE LETTER TO CREDITORS

Date

Name
Address
City, State, Zip Code

Re: ______________________________, deceased; Date of Death: ______________; Account No.: ______________

Dear Sir/Madam,

This is to inform you of the death of the above. I believe that his/her loan (account) is covered by a life insurance plan through your company to pay off any unpaid balance. Please refer to your records and inform me of the proper steps I need to take to insure payment.

Thank you for your assistance.

Sincerely,

(Signature)

Your name
Address
City, State, Zip Code

SAMPLE LETTER TO DECEASED'S EMPLOYER

Date

Name of Employer
Address
City, State, Zip Code

Re: ____, deceased;
Employer I.D. # ________________________

Dear Sir/Madam,

This is to inform you officially that my (husband, wife, etc.) died on (date). Please send me information on any available benefits such as group life insurance, pension plan, accrued vacation or sick benefits, terminal pay allowances, gratuity payments, service recognition award, unpaid commissions, disability pay, credit union balance, stock purchase or profit sharing plans, etc.

Please send me the required documents and forms that must be completed by the beneficiary of these benefits.

Sincerely,

(Signature)

Your name
Address
City, State, Zip Code

SAMPLE LETTER TO SOCIAL SECURITY, VETERANS ADMINISTRATION, CIVIL SERVICE, RAILROAD WORKERS

Date

Department of Health, Education & Welfare (or appropriate agency)
Social Security Administration Payment Center
Address
City, State, Zip Code

Re: ______________________________, deceased; Date of Death: __________________; Identification Number (if known): __________________

Dear Sir/Madam,

I am the estate representative of the above-named person. Enclosed is the decedent's check for the month of ____________, which is being returned as required. Please acknowledge receipt of the enclosed check by signing the duplicate copy of this letter, and returning it to me in the enclosed stamped self-addressed envelope.

Sincerely,

(Signature)

Your name
Address
City, State, Zip Code

RECEIPT ACKNOWLEDGED BY:

____
(Name)

____
(Title)

____
(Date)

SAMPLE LETTER TO CREDIT CARD COMPANY

Date

Name of Credit Card Company or Creditor
Address
City, State, Zip Code

Re:_________________________________, deceased; Date of death: ______________

Dear Sir/Madam,

I am the representative of the above named decedent.

Enclosed you will find credit card (number) ____________, which has been cut in half, and should be immediately cancelled. Please acknowledge receipt of the card (or this letter) by signing the duplicate copy of this letter and returning it to me in the enclosed stamped self-addressed envelope.

-OR-

Dear Sir/Madam,

I am the above-named decedent's spouse and wish to have account number ________________ changed to the name of (your name) ________________________. Please acknowledge receipt of this letter by signing the duplicate copy and returning it to me in the enclosed stamped self-addressed envelope.

Sincerely,

(Signature)

Your name
Address
City, State, Zip Code

(Continued, next page)

RECEIPT ACKNOWLEDGED BY:

____
(Name)

____
(Title)

____
(Date)

SAMPLE LETTER TO CONTEST BILLING

Date

Billing/Credit Department
Name of Company
Address
City, State, Zip Code

Dear Sir/Madam,

I am writing to contest the bill from your company dated (   ). See enclosed photocopy of the bill in question.

This merchandise was not ordered by me. I do not expect further correspondence from you unless you can provide me with documentation of an order placed by me.

Sincerely,

(Signature)

Your name
Address
City, State, Zip Code

Enclosure

cc: Federal Trade Commission
U.S. Postal Service

SAMPLE LETTER TO BROKER OR INVESTMENT COMPANY

Date

Name of Broker or Investment Company
Address
City, State, Zip Code

Re: ________________________________, deceased; Account No.(s): ________________________, ________________________

Dear Sir/Madam or Name,

This letter is written to inform you that my (husband, wife, etc.) died on (day, month, year). Will you please send correspondence concerning the account(s) to me at the address below? I will contact you re further activity and/or disposition of this account.

Sincerely,

(Signature)

Your name
Address
City, State, Zip Code

SAMPLE LETTER TO TRANSFER SECURITIES

Date

Name of Brokerage House & Broker
Address
City, State, Zip Code

Re: ______________________________, deceased; Date of Death: ____________

Dear Sir/Madam,

This is to notify you that the above named person died on the date indicated.

The decedent's records indicate that he/she was the owner of securities/investments in the following account(s).

Account # ________________ , #____________________

Please advise of the documentation you will require to transfer title to the new owner(s). If you do not currently act as tranfer agent for the company, please advise the name and address of the current transfer agent.

Please acknowledge receipt of this letter by signing the duplicate copy of this letter, and returning it to me in the enclosed stamped self-addressed envelope.

Thank you for your assistance.

Sincerely,

(Signature)

Your name
Your Address
City, State, Zip Code

RECEIPT ACKNOWLEDGED BY:

____
(Name)

____
(Title)

____
(Date)

SAMPLE LETTER RE CHANGE OF OWNERSHIP

Date

Name of Individual or Institution
(e.g. Bank, Brokerage Co.)
Address
City, State, Zip Code

Re: ______________________________, deceased; Date of Death:________Identification No. (s) :______________

Dear Sir/Madam,

Enclosed please find a copy of the death certificate for the person named above. Please send me the appropriate documents and instruction to be completed for change of ownership.

Sincerely,

(Signature)

Name
Address
City, State, Zip Code

SAMPLE LETTER TO M.D. OR HEALTH CARE INSTITUTION TO BILL DIRECTLY TO MEDICARE

Date

Name of M.D. or Health Care Institution
Address
City, State, Zip Code

Re:_______________________________, deceased; Date of Death:
____

Dear Sir/Madam,

This letter is written to inform you that my (husband, wife, etc.) is deceased. I have enclosed the bill(s) for service that were sent to the deceased's address. Please send the bill directly to Medicare.

When the bill for service has been paid by Medicare, please notify me at the address below if there is further payment due.

Sincerely,

(Signature)

Your name
Address
City, State, Zip Code

SAMPLE LETTER TO THE BUREAU OF VITAL STATISTICS

Date

Bureau of Vital Statistics
(Your local county)
Address
City, State, Zip Code

Re:_______________________________________,deceased;
Date of Death:____________________________,City and County
of death:____

Dear Sir/Madam,

Please provide me with (number) certified copies of the death certificate for the above-named decedent. A check in the amount of ______________ and a self-addressed, stamped envelope are enclosed.

Thank you for your assistance.

Sincerely,

(Signature)

Your name
Address
City, State, Zip Code

Enclosure

SAMPLE LETTER RE ORGAN DONATION

Date

Dear ______________________,

In case of accidental or natural death, I wish to donate the following (e.g. corneas, kidneys, heart, or current need) or my body to the (institution) or to medical science. Presently, I carry a Uniform Donor Card in my (wallet or billfold). On the card, specific instructions are defined. I wish to have these instructions followed at my death.

If the card is not available, please see that the proper individual(s) or institution is notified of my wishes re organ donation. This letter may be used as verification of my intentions.

Sincerely

(Signature)

Printed or Typewritten Name
Address
City, State, Zip Code

SAMPLE LETTER OF COMPLAINT

Date

Appropriate Department/Person
Organization
Street address
City, State, Zip Code

Re: (product, date, place of purchase, serial #, model #, Law, Event)

Dear Sir/Madam,

This letter is written regarding the situation noted above. I am concerned because (describe problem briefly, and note enclosed copies of bills, contracts, cancelled check(s), sales receipts, newspaper articles, hearing notices, etc.).

I have tried to resolve this problem by the following actions (list actions and dates).

I will expect action or resolution of this problem within 30 days of receipt of this letter. I thank you in advance for your assistance.

Sincerely,

(Signature)

Name
Address
City, State, Zip Code

Enclosures

cc: (Names of Organization/Persons receiving copies of this letter)

SAMPLE LETTER OF CONSENT FOR TREATMENT/ MEDICAL CARE OF A MINOR

To Whom It May Concern:

(I) (We) the undersigned, parent(s)/person having legal custody/legal guardian of ______________________________, a minor, hereby authorize ______________________________ as the agent(s) for the undersigned to consent to any X-ray examination, anesthetic, medical or surgical diagnosis or treatment, and hospital care which is deemed necessary by, and is to be rendered under the general or special supervision of, any physician and/or surgeon licensed under the provisions of the Medical Practice Act on medical staff of any hospital, whether such diagnosis or treatment is rendered at the office of said physician or at said hospital.

It is understood that this authorization is given in advance of any specific diagnosis, treatment or hospital care being required but is given to provide authority and power on part of the aforesaid agent(s) to give specific consent to any and all such diagnosis, treatment, or hospital care which a physician, may, in the exercise of his/her best judgement deem necessary.

This authorization is given pursuant to the provisions of Section 25.8 of the Civil Code of California (seek appropriate Civil Code in your State).

(I) (We) hereby authorize any hospital which has provided to the above-named minor pursuant to the provisions of the Civil Code referred to above to surrender physical custody of such minor to (my) (our) above-named agent upon the completion of treatment. The authorization is given pursuant to Section 1283 of the Health and Safety Code of California (seek appropriate Health and Safety Code in your State, if existent).

These authorizations shall remain effective until ________, 19____, unless sooner revoked in writing to said agent(s).

Date: ____________________ ______________________________

Parent

____

Legal Guardian

____

Person Having Legal Custody

INDEX

NOTES

NOTES

NOTES

NOTES

NOTES

NOTES

NOTES

NOTES

NOTES

NOTES